Cloud Computing

From Beginning to End

Cloud Technology, Design, and Migration
Methodologies Explained

Ray Rafaels

rrafaels@axcendinc.com

Cloud Computing
From Beginning to End
2nd Edition 2.6
Copyright © 2018 Ray Rafaels
ISBN-13: 978-1986726283
ISBN-10: 1986726282

Ray Rafaels can be contacted at rrafaels@axcendinc.com

Contents

List of Figures

List of Tables

Preface

Cloud computing is today's favorite buzzword that almost everyone hears, but very few truly understand. What is clear, however, is that cloud technology and services are poised to redefine the Information Technology (IT) landscape and improve the way the government, Department of Defense (DoD), and companies operate.

This book covers not only the technical details of how public and private cloud technology works, but also the strategy, technical design, and in-depth implementation details required to migrate existing applications to the cloud. After reading this book, you will have a much better understanding of cloud technology and the steps required to quickly reap its benefits, while at the same time lowering your IT implementation risk.

Target Audience

This book was written for a diverse group of management, information technology, and information security professionals including:

- IT management - CIOs, senior level information technology managers, and program managers within the government, DoD, and commercial sectors.
- IT development - Software developers, system architects, and systems integrators.
- Cyber security assessment and monitoring - System evaluators, assessors, independent verifiers/validators, auditors, analysts, system administrators, database administrators, and information system owners.
- Software and hardware sales professionals.

Acknowledgements

I would like to thank my lovely wife, Nadine Rafaels, and the rest of my family, who supported and encouraged me in spite of all the time it took me away from them. I thank Sandi Mathers for the professional editing and formatting of this latest v2.6 Edition. Her keen eye and many years of technical writing and editing expertise were essential in making this book a further success. I would also like to thank Brad Moore for his professional editing on the previous v1 and v2 Editions of this book. His excellent technical and business skills were key assets in making this book an original success.

1. Definition of the Cloud

Many people and organizations have defined cloud computing slightly different. You probably see the definitions in online news articles, blogs, presentations, etc. The simple and short definition that I typically use is, "Cloud computing is the self-provisioning and on-demand delivery of IT resources and applications over the Internet with a pay-as-you-go pricing model."

The official definition of cloud computing is provided by the National Institute of Standards and Technology's (NIST) in *The NIST Definition of Cloud Computing, Special Publication 800-145*. This publication is summarized in the next section and is also posted at www.nist.gov.

NIST Definition of Cloud Computing[1]

NIST has defined cloud computing as, ".... a model for enabling ubiquitous, convenient, on-demand network access to a shared pool of configurable computing resources (e.g., networks, servers, storage, applications and services) that can be rapidly provisioned and released with minimal management effort or service provider interaction."

NIST
National Institute of
Standards and Technology
U.S. Department of Commerce

Figure 1 NIST Emblem

---

[1] Reprinted courtesy of the National Institute of Standards and Technology, U.S. Department of Commerce. Not copyrightable in the United States.

Peter Mell and Timothy Grance of NIST documented the NIST definition in Publication 800-145. I ran into Peter Mell at a NIST conference a few years ago and asked him if he gets a lot of questions on his cloud definition document. It is interesting to note that Peter said that he was very surprised that his simple 3-page document generated so much attention. He also said that the *Definition of Cloud Computing* document is what everyone seems to know him for. He concluded by saying that the attention is great, but he preferred to be remembered by one of his more complex and detailed works at NIST.

NIST's *Definition of Cloud Computing* document lists five essential characteristics of cloud computing:

- On-demand self-service
- Broad network access
- Resource pooling
- Rapid elasticity or expansion
- Measured service

This document also lists three service models and four deployment models[2].

---

[2] Reprinted courtesy of the National Institute of Standards and Technology, U.S. Department of Commerce. Not copyrightable in the United States.

The following figure illustrates the NIST detailed definition of cloud computing.

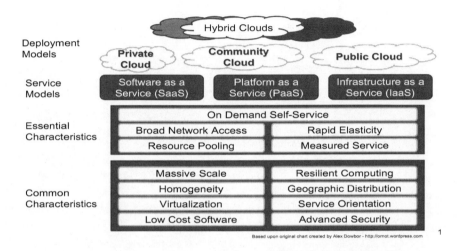

Figure 2 NIST Cloud Computing Definition Illustration

To better understand the definition of cloud computing, the following table defines some important people or groups that are involved with cloud computing.

Table 1 Cloud Actor Definitions

Actor Name	Description
Cloud Consumer or User	A person who is authenticated to a Cloud Service Provider (CSP) and uses cloud services.
CSP (CSP)	A public or private cloud provider that delivers cloud infrastructure services over the Internet (e.g., Amazon AWS, Google, Microsoft Azure, etc.).
Cloud Managed Service or Consulting Provider	An IT services company that assists agencies/companies with designing, deploying, operating, and supporting cloud programs.
Cloud Subscriber	A person or organization that has been authenticated to a cloud and maintains a business relationship with a cloud.

The following subsections describe the five essential characteristics of cloud computing.

On-Demand, Self-Service

A consumer can unilaterally provision computing capabilities, such as server time and network storage, as needed automatically without requiring human interaction with each service provider.

Broad Network Access

Capabilities are available over the network and accessed through standard mechanisms that promote use by heterogeneous thin or thick client platforms (e.g., mobile phones, tablets, laptops, and workstations).

Resource Pooling

The cloud provider's computing resources are pooled to serve multiple consumers using a multi-tenant model, with different physical and virtual resources dynamically assigned and reassigned according to consumer demand. There is a sense of location independence in that the customer generally has no control or knowledge over the exact location of the provided resources, but may be able to specify location at a higher level of abstraction (e.g., country, state, or data center). Examples of resources include storage, processing, memory, and network bandwidth.

Rapid Elasticity

Capabilities can be elastically provisioned and released in some cases automatically to scale rapidly outward and inward commensurate with demand. To the consumer, the capabilities available for provisioning often appear to be unlimited and can be appropriated in any quantity at any time.

Measured Service

Cloud systems automatically control and optimize resource use by leveraging a metering capability at some level of abstraction appropriate to the type of service (e.g., storage, processing, bandwidth, and active user accounts). Resource usage can be monitored, controlled, and reported, providing transparency for both the provider and consumer of the utilized service.

Summary

The cloud computing description in this section is supposed to be the official definition that we all use. With the current cloud "hype" in the marketplace today, anything "cloud" is good. As such, I have found many government, DoD, and commercial representatives stretching the cloud definition. For example, most people claim their IT infrastructure is "cloud based" as long as it uses server virtualization, even though their enterprise does not deliver the five essential cloud characteristics listed in Figure 2.

Now that we have defined what cloud computing is, the following subsections describe the various cloud-based service models that can be utilized.

Software as a Service (SaaS)

The capability provided to the consumer is to use the cloud provider's applications running on its cloud infrastructure. The applications are accessible from various client devices through either a thin client interface, such as a web browser (e.g., web-based email) or program interface. The consumer does not manage or control the underlying cloud infrastructure including the network, servers, Operating Systems (OSs), storage, or even individual application capabilities, with the possible exception of limited user-specific application configuration settings.

Most people have used cloud computing services and probably didn't realize it. Anyone who has used Gmail or Hotmail has already used a Software as a Service (SaaS) cloud-based service. The email software and storage doesn't exist on your computer; it is located in the cloud.

Platform as a Service (PaaS)

The capability provided to the consumer is a pre-installed cloud infrastructure platform, such as a relational database environment, Hadoop big data, Java development, etc. Platform as a Service (PaaS) is created using programming languages, libraries, services, and tools supported by the provider. The consumer does not manage or control the underlying cloud infrastructure including the network, servers, OSs, or storage, but has control over the deployed applications and possibly configuration settings for the application-hosting environment.

Infrastructure as a Service (IaaS)

The capability provided to the consumer is to provision processing, storage, networks, and other fundamental computing resources where the consumer is able to deploy and run arbitrary software, which can include OSs and applications. With Infrastructure as a Service (IaaS), the consumer does not manage or control the underlying cloud infrastructure, but has control over OSs, storage, and deployed applications—and possibly limited control of select networking components (e.g., host firewalls).

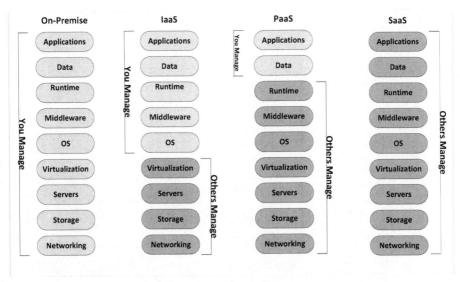

Figure 3 Types of Cloud Services

The following subsections describe the cloud deployment models.

Private Cloud

The private cloud infrastructure is provisioned for exclusive use by a single organization comprising of multiple consumers (e.g., business units). It can be owned, managed, and operated by the organization, a third party, or some combination of them, and it may exist on or off premises.

Community Cloud

The community cloud infrastructure is provisioned for exclusive use by a specific community of consumers from organizations that have shared concerns (e.g., mission, security requirements, policy, and compliance considerations). This cloud can be owned, managed, and operated by one or more of the organizations in the community, a third party, or some combination of them, and it may exist on or off premises.

Public Cloud

The public cloud infrastructure is provisioned for open use by the general public. This cloud can be owned, managed, and operated by a business, an academic, or a government organization, or some combination of them, and it exists on the premises of the cloud provider.

Hybrid Cloud

The hybrid cloud infrastructure is a composition of two or more distinct cloud infrastructures (private, community, or public) that remain unique entities, but are bound together by standardized or proprietary technology that enables data and application portability (e.g., cloud bursting for load balancing between clouds).

Cloud Benefits

The following lists the benefits of cloud computing and why someone would want to rely on it for their computing needs:

- **Reduces capital costs** - No need to pay upfront costs for hardware, software, and associated maintenance.
- **Scalability** - Quickly increases capacity and productivity with less people.
- **Quicker time-to-market** -Decrease the time it takes to provision an IT infrastructure, thereby speeding the delivery of IT projects.
- **Less personnel training** - Less training for technical personnel, since less people are required for operations.
- **Increased agility** - Change direction quickly with regard to infrastructure design and scalability.

- **Mobility** - Access the applications anywhere in the world as long as an Internet connection is available. Data is accessible through shared storage (i.e., a storage area network) and is not stuck on a hard drive within a single server.
- **Reduced data center facility costs** - Less costs in the data center since the processing and storage have been moved to the cloud.
- **Simplify capacity planning** - Less time and money is spent on analyzing and scaling up your IT infrastructure. Capacity can be easily scaled up or down in response to changing workloads.

Most people I talk to identify cost savings, scalability, and quicker time-to-market as the top three key benefits for cloud computing. A more scientific survey was performed in 2017 by Vanson Bourne (Research Company) for government and commercial clients, and it shows a slightly different priority list of cloud benefits for clients (see the following figure).

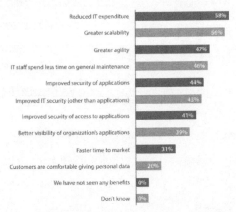

Figure 4 Cloud Benefits Survey 2017[3]

---

[3] Vanson Bourne, 6/22/2017, https://www.vansonbourne.com/client-research/21111601TC.

This survey shows cost, scalability, and agility as the top three reasons to move to the cloud. Whatever your reasons are to consider moving to the cloud, it is always a good idea to perform a cost benefit analysis. The analysis steps are described in "Return on Investment (ROI)."

Before we go into a detailed description of cloud computing, it is best to first understand the technologies that make it possible. Let's start from the beginning and examine the origins of cloud computing.

A Little History—What technologies led us to the cloud?

Is cloud computing really a new business model in the computing world? Some say application hosting performed by Application Service Providers (ASPs) in the 90's is similar to today's SaaS cloud computing model. Although the hosting may have been similar, the ASP model typically involved delivering the application services using separate single-tenant (or client) instances. This meant they did not leverage the cost benefits of multi-tenancy or multiple clients on a single server, since cloud technology was not available at the time. What is different today is the use of a technology called "virtualization." Virtualization decouples computer hardware, OSs, data, applications, and user states across the physical enterprise infrastructure.

2. Cloud Technology

Virtualization is a Key Technology

The most common way to virtualize your IT environment is through the use of a piece of software called a "hypervisor" that creates and runs Virtual Machines (VMs). A VM is a piece of software that runs an OS and applications, just like a real physical computer. A computer on which a hypervisor is running a VM is called a "host."

Although virtualization was used by IBM in the late 60's and early 70's on mainframe computers, virtualization for today's x86-based servers didn't occur until the late 90's through products from Connectix and VMware. Virtualization is a key technology for cloud computing because it provides a layer of abstraction between the computing, storage, network interface, and applications running on it. It also provides scalability and emulates a computer system so multiple OSs can run on a single server. Because of this separation, virtualization permits automatic online migration to a secondary physical server if the first server becomes overloaded or fails.

The following figure illustrates three VMs or computer systems on one physical computer.

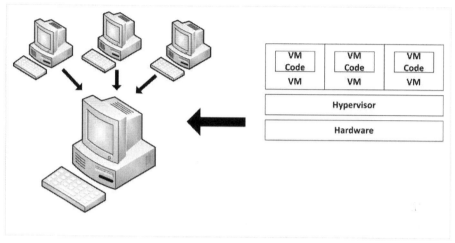

Figure 5 Illustration of Three Separate VMs Installed on One Computer

Hypervisors can be installed in two different ways to provide virtualization—native and hosted.

Native

Native hypervisor software runs directly on a host's hardware and has direct access to hardware resources, which is sometimes referred to as a "bare metal" installation. This software provides a layer of abstraction separating the hardware and OSs. Bare metal virtualization usually results in better performance, scalability, and stability. One disadvantage is that the hypervisor must have the necessary device drivers for the server hardware.

Hosted

Hosted hypervisor software runs on top of an OS like Windows Server 20xx, Linux, and Unix as a distinct software layer. Other OSs run at the third level above the hardware.

The following figure illustrates a computer system before and after a bare metal hypervisor installation.

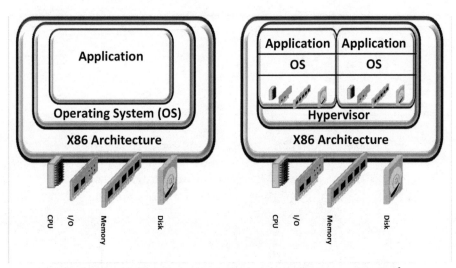

Figure 6 Computer System before and after Virtualization[4]

As mentioned earlier in this section, virtualization is performed using a hypervisor. Hypervisor software can create a VM (VM), which is a fully functioning virtual computer that has an OS, network configuration, and application software.

---

[4] VMware, virtualization overview white paper. 2018.
https://www.vmware.com/solutions/virtualization.htm

Containers

Containers are a newer virtualization technology used in the cloud industry. The key difference between containers and VMs is that while a hypervisor abstracts an entire device, containers abstract just the OS kernel.

Containers make it much easier to package and move programs into different cloud environments. One difference to note between VMs and containers is that VMs are based upon emulating virtual computer hardware, which causes more processing cycles for managing computing, memory, and storage requirements.

There are pros and cons for each type of virtualization technology. While VMs provide more isolation with guaranteed resources, containers isolate processes from each other, but allow more applications to be run on a host since it uses fewer resources.

In contrast, containers use shared OSs, which means they are much more efficient than VMs. Greater efficiency allows you to run more server applications on the same hardware. For example, if you are using an open source container technology such as Docker, when you make changes to the base OS, it commits those changes and creates an image. This image contains only the differences from the base OS. When the OS is run, it uses the base image and an image of the changes.

The AnotherUnionFS (AUFS) file system is used by Docker and layers the change image on top of the base using a layered file system. AUFS merges the different layers together, creating an OS with all the changes intact and operational. As more changes are made, the images are saved and layered on top of the OS. The following figure illustrates the difference between containers (Docker) and VMs.

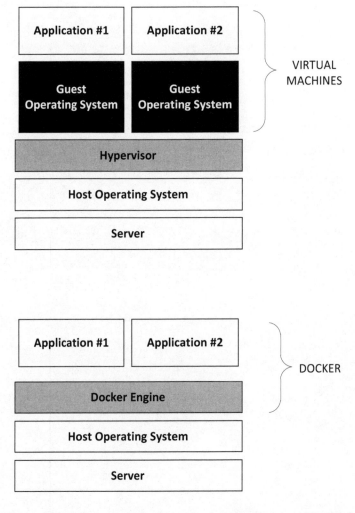

Figure 7 Differences between VMs and Containers (Docker)

Are Containers New?

Containers are actually not new; they date back to the year 2000. Back then, Oracle (Sun) Solaris container technology was introduced and is today called "Zones." Since Oracle zones are reported to be difficult to configure and use, they have failed to gain a wide following. Google has its own open source container technology called Let Me Contain That For You (lmctfy). Anytime you use Google Search, Gmail, or Google Docs, you are using containers.

Docker is becoming popular because it makes container technology easier and less costly to deploy. Containers also have the benefit of saving you money on OS software. With VMs, you need a separate OS for each VM, which can cost more money.

Containers make applications very portable. To help with management, Google developed "Kubernetes," which is a system for managing containerized applications across a cluster of nodes. This comes in handy for developers and system administrators when they want to move applications between development, test, and production environments. It also makes it easier to not get "locked into" a particular cloud provider. In addition, since Red Hat, Microsoft, Google, and Amazon AWS are supporting Docker, it is starting to look like it will be the go-to standard for container technology. For the purpose of this book, we will focus on the use of VMs within cloud environments since this technology is currently more widespread.

Virtualization and VM Portability

One of the slickest features of virtualization is the ability to move live or archived VMs. This move can be accomplished using popular hypervisors such as VMware, Hyper-V, and Citrix. Public clouds such as Amazon AWS, Microsoft Azure, and Google Cloud use custom-developed or open source hypervisors.

The following table lists the hypervisor types used by each public cloud.

Table 2 Public Cloud Providers and Hypervisor Types Used

Public Cloud	Hypervisor Used
Amazon AWS	Amazon Machine Image (AMI) is a custom design based off of Citrix Xen.
Microsoft Azure	Azure Hypervisor (customized version of Hyper-V)
Google Cloud	Linux Containers

The benefits of VM portability include:

- Moving VMs to new hardware (Compute, Storage, etc.) for tech upgrades.
- Balancing the load across hosts (manual and automatically).
- Fast provisioning for development, test, and production environments.
- Disaster recovery and Continuity of Operations Planning (COOP) activities.

Most of the hypervisor vendors use the same general technique to move a VM between physical host computers.

Figure 8 on the next page illustrates the movement of a VM from Host 1 to Host 2. In this example, both hosts share the same network subnet and storage. The use of shared storage allows for a faster VM transfer rate since the stored VM software and configurations are already accessible on the shared storage. The VM on Host 2 can just load the VM software from the shared storage instead of waiting for it to be transferred from Host 1. The only thing left is to load the memory state bitmap of the VM on Host 1, which is transferred over the network to the VM on Host 2. When the bitmap has been transferred, the user is then switched to the new VM and the original VM is removed from Host 1.

As you can see, the entire VM is not actually moved, just the memory state of the VM on Host 1. If shared storage was not used in the architecture, then the entire contents of the VM would need to be moved. Because moving the entire contents of a VM takes much longer than just the memory contents, most designs try to leverage the use of shared storage from a Storage Area Network (SAN) or Software-Defined Storage (SDS).

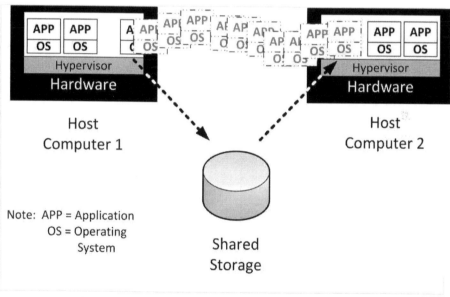

Figure 8 Movement of a VM from Host 1 to Host 2

Depending upon your VM type, some of the following restrictions need to be addressed:

- Use of shared storage
- Access to the same network
- Compatible CPUs

Which VM Software is Right for You?

Confused over which VM software to use? You are not alone. So which one is the best? Any good consultant will tell you that "it depends." (Don't you hate that response?) But honestly, it does depend on your requirements, budget, and current environment. Over the years, I have observed the types of VM solutions that government agencies and commercial companies have gravitated towards. This is not a scientific survey, but I have summarized my personal observations in the following table.

Table 3 Agency/Business Profile and VM Typically Used

| Government Agency or Company Profile | VM Typically Purchased | | | |
	VMware VSphere	Microsoft Hyper-V	Red Hat KVM	Citrix Xen
Microsoft Heavy Organization	X	X		
Budget Conscious Organization			X	X
Wants "Feature Rich" Solution and Budget is Not Really an issue	X			
Prefer Open Source Solutions			X	
Currently Using Citrix Thin Client Solutions				X
Prefer to Go with the Industry Leader	X			

Table 3 gives an insight as to what others have done, but to find the right solution for your organization, a detailed assessment of your requirements and goals should be documented and linked to your IT architecture. A full discussion of this process is described in the "Design" section in Chapter 4. In the meantime, I have summarized some of the key features of the more popular hypervisor solutions in a comparative matrix (shown in Table 4 on the next page). This table will help shed light on the technology differences that best drive your solution.

Table 4 Key Features of Popular Hypervisor Solutions[5]

VM (Hypervisor) Feature	Hypervisor Software			
	VMware VSphere	**Microsoft Hyper-V**	**Red Hat KVM**	**Citrix Xen**
Management	Yes, vCenter Server, extra cost	System Center, extra cost	Must pay a subscription for Red Hat Enterprise Virtualizatio n (RHEV)	Free
Automated Live Migration	Yes	Yes	Yes	No
Cluster Size	Max 32 hosts, 4000 VMs	Max 64 Hosts, 8000 VMs	200 Hosts/ clusters	16 Hosts
Max CPU/Host (Logical)	320	320	160	160
Maximum Memory/Host	4TB	4TB	4TB	1TB
Open Virtualization Format (OVF) Support	Yes	Yes	Yes	Yes

---

[5] Used with permission from www.WhatMatrix.com.

VM (Hypervisor) Feature	Hypervisor Software			
	VMware VSphere	Microsoft Hyper-V	Red Hat KVM	Citrix Xen
Maximum Disk Space	62TB (VMDK)	64TB (VHDX)	8TB	2TB
Private VLAN	Yes	Yes	No	Yes
VM Patching	limited	Yes	Yes	No

Cloud Storage

Cloud storage is a model of data storage where digital data is remotely accessed, stored, maintained, and backed up. Users gain access to the data over the internet or private network connection. Cloud storage can be obtained from public clouds such as Amazon AWS S3, Microsoft Azure, and Google. These public clouds offer services in a multi-tenant environment. Private cloud storage services can be provided in dedicated environments and protected behind an agency or company's firewall.

Hybrid cloud storage is a combination of public and private storage, and typically includes a Virtual Private Network (VPN) tunnel between the private and public clouds. A common example of a hybrid model is to have active data in your private cloud and archival data shipped off to the public cloud (e.g., Amazon AWS Glacier storage, Microsoft Azure, or Google Cloud services).

Storage Area Network (SAN)

Within the cloud, the underlying storage technologies typically used are SANs and SDS. The Storage Networking Industry Association (SNIA) defines a SAN as, "... any high-performance network whose primary purpose is to enable storage devices to communicate with computer systems and with each other."

Typically a SAN consists of any array of hard disks connected through a control and fiber channel or iSCSI switches. A SAN connects to the servers in such a way that the devices appear as locally attached to the OS. The SAN allows multiple servers to access potentially any area of the storage. The benefits of a SAN include:

- **Management:** SAN can remotely assign storage to a server with no downtime.
- **Availability:** SAN storage is typically more reliable than a Direct-Attached Storage (DAS) disk.
- **Disk utilization:** DAS storage is more wasteful since extra storage on one server cannot be easily shared with another server (unless you use SDS).
- **Backup:** SAN can use snapshots and data replication for centralizing backup and recovery.

The best way to understand the benefits and see the operation of a SAN is to review Figure 9 and Figure 10 on the following pages.

Figure 9 shows rack-mountable servers each with internal hard disk storage. Since the data contained on each internal drive is separated, data needs to be copied to the other computers for all the VMs to have shared read and write access to the data.

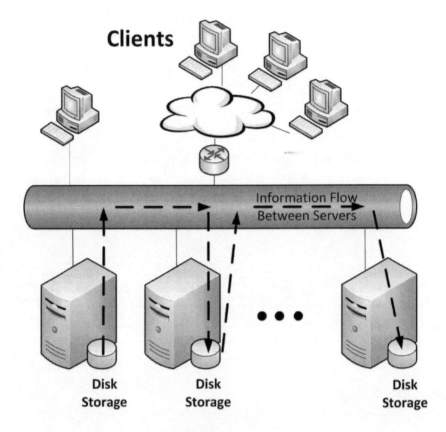

Figure 9 Shared Storage Challenges with Separate Disks in Non-SAN Environment

In Figure 10, the computers are connected to a SAN-based architecture. With a SAN, all of the servers have connectivity to all of the underlying data storage (configuration management is used to allow or deny final access). If Server A needs data that was produced by Server B, it can access the storage directly—there is no need to copy data from Server A to Server B.

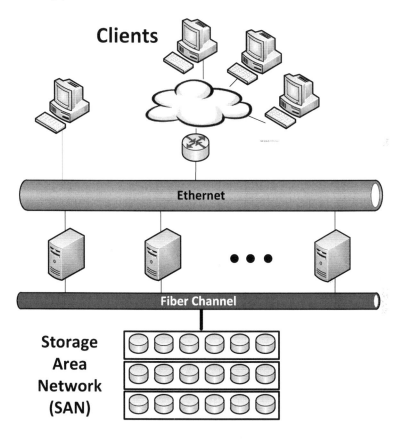

Figure 10 Shared Storage Access Using a SAN

Software-Designed Storage (SDS)

As previously described, SANs are able to *replace* individual disk drives in servers with a centrally-managed pool of shared storage. This removed the issue of having many disconnected underutilized disk drives, locked in server enclosures, primarily servicing their own local server. Another way of solving this issue is to create an SDS solution that actually taps into these local server drives, abstracts the storage from the physical devices, and provides accessibility to all servers in the storage cluster. Some SDS solutions can also tie in legacy storage solutions such as SAN and Network Attached Storage (NAS) as part of an overall SDS solution.

SDS has the same benefits as a SAN, with the added benefit of a centralized management capability that cuts across *heterogeneous* storage devices and has the ability to scale horizontally (no need to add new hardware storage controllers). On the other hand, the benefit of a SAN is that you know in advance that everything was designed and tested to work together. With SDS (most of the time), you are creating your storage network on-the-fly. Also, your SAN support is greatly simplified since one vendor typically provides the support. This can be viewed as a benefit to many understaffed IT organizations.

How SDS Works

The first thing most people think about when they hear about SDS is, how can a read/write operation on a VM (or server) occur fast enough when the disk drive storage is located across the network on another server's disk drive? The answer is Solid State Drive (SSD) read/write caching. An SSD is much faster than a slow, spinning disk drive. SSDs are data storage devices that have no magnetic spinning disk drives, and are composed entirely of integrated circuit memory.

The SSDs constructed today have NAND-based flash memory, which retains data without power.

The storage latency is minimized by accelerating read/write disk I/O traffic through fast SSDs. The VM performance is improved by leveraging the flash as both a write buffer and a read cache. All write I/Os go to the SSD first, and are eventually moved to the disk drives automatically.

Most read and all write transactions must travel across a network. Because caching is distributed across multiple servers, a dedicated network is required to provide the highest possible performance (e.g., 10Gbps). To protect against SSD or server failure, data is also stored on an SSD located on a different server. At regular intervals, the write data in the SSDs are moved to disk drives. In the event of a server failure, the copy of the buffered or stored data on the other server ensures that no data loss occurs.

The following figure shows the SDS Virtual San Solution (VSAN) solution from VMware.

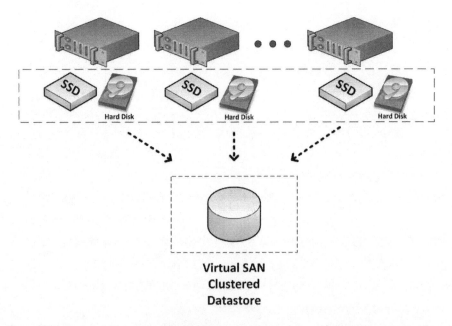

**Virtual SAN
Clustered
Datastore**

Figure 11 SDS Virtual San Solution (VSAN) Solution from VMware[6]

When a physical server is configured to use a SAN, the host OS treats the SAN as if it were a storage device, such as a disk volume assigned to a local drive letter. Because the host OS can access the storage device, you can place all files associated with the VMs on the SAN. The SAN provides all storage and the physical server that runs the VMs provides the memory and CPU resources.

---

[6] Rivera, Rawlinson. "VMware vSphere Blog. Begin the journey to a private cloud with data center virtualization." Web. 9 April 2014. Used with permission from VMware.

Load Balancers

Load balancers automatically distribute incoming application traffic across multiple VM hosts. Load balancing enables you to achieve fault tolerance, as well as scalability. Amazon AWS, Google, and Microsoft all provide load balancing as part of their public cloud offering. Their load balancing features are contained within the Elastic Load Balancing (ELB), Google Compute Engine, and Azure load balancer (network level), respectively.

Public cloud monitoring capabilities check the health of the VMs. When unhealthy VMs are detected, traffic is no longer routed to them. Traffic is spread across all of the remaining operational VMs. The load balancer can be set up to route traffic to geographically-dispersed VMs (availability zones) to enhance availability. When the unhealthy VMs are repaired and become operational, the load balancer resumes routing traffic to those instances.

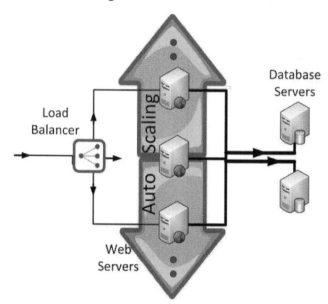

Figure 12 Cloud-Based Load Balancer

The benefit of public cloud load balancers is that they simplify the complexity of configuring, managing, and scaling of load balancers. The service is designed to automatically add and remove capacity as needed, without manual intervention.

How Load Balancers Work

Load balancers monitor traffic and handle requests that come in through the Internet. There is a management component that monitors the load balancers, adds and removes capacity as needed, and verifies that the load balancers are behaving properly.

Per Figure 13 and Figure 14 on the following pages, below describes the basic load balancing data transfer steps.

1. The client sends a URL request to DNS servers to access the application.
2. The DNS servers return the IP addresses of the load balancer.
3. The client computer (end user) sends a packet to the load balancer.
4. The load balancer grabs the packet, decides which host should receive the packet (Host A), and changes the destination IP address to Host A.
5. Host A accepts the packet and responds back.
6. The load balancer grabs the packet from Host A, changes the source IP to the load balancer, and forwards the packet back to the client.
7. The client, load balancer, and host continue to send/receive data.

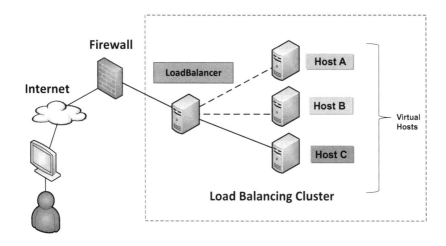

Figure 13 Load Balancer Example

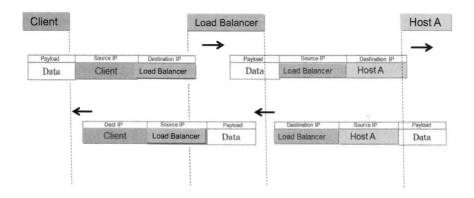

Figure 14 Load Balancer Data Flow between Client and Host A

The DNS record should be configured with a Time-to-Live (TTL) setting of 60 seconds to force the clients to again look up the DNS at least every 60 seconds. This setting ensures that the load balancer IP address is provided in case the load balancer moves.

Secure Socket Layer (SSL) Traffic and Load Balancers

The Secure Socket Layer (SSL) is a cryptographic protocol designed to provide secure connectivity over the Internet. SSL encrypts data being passed between the client computer and website. Browsers show *https:://* and a small picture of a lock when the site is using SSL. The web server that holds the SSL certificate decrypts the data. Alternatively, some load balancers can be configured to decrypt the data using the SSL certificate to lessen the load on the web servers.

Session "Stickiness"

Many times when a user is browsing through a site, session data is maintained using cookies. In this case, it is important for the user to always use the same host server in the load balancing cluster during the session. The load balancer is responsible for ensuring that the "sticky" session is maintained.

For example, if a user is trying to purchase an item at a website such as www.example.com, there can be several steps included in the session. The user needs to add the item to the shopping cart, enter the billing information, check out, and then complete the sale. During this session, the user needs to connect to the same server for each step, or the transaction can never be completed.

Auto Scaling with Elastic Load Balancing (ELB)

Load balancers can be coupled with public cloud auto scaling features to ensure the front-end and back-end systems have sufficient capacity for varying levels of traffic. Within Amazon AWS, if you want to ensure that the number of healthy Elastic Compute Cloud (EC2) instances behind an Elastic Load Balancer is between a minimum of two (2) and a maximum of five (5), you can configure Auto Scaling to meet this requirement. When Auto Scaling detects that more computing resources are needed, it automatically adds more EC2 instances to the Auto Scaling Group. Auto Scaling works well whether you are using ELB or not.

Large-scale applications with high user traffic require multiple servers and VM instances. Estimating the number of IT infrastructure resources can be tricky. Most people design their infrastructure to handle what they believe their peak load might be, even if it is infrequent. This is not a cost-efficient approach since most of the IT resources will have low utilization during normal operation. Another approach is to provision for average use. Although this is more cost effective, it delivers poor performance when the load increases above the average.

Auto Scaling can solve these problems. When the load increases, Auto Scaling provisions more resources to handle the increased demand. The result is high performance, regardless of the user demand. Auto Scaling manages the launch and termination of VMs on your behalf.

3. Cloud Security

A major portion of this section on cloud security was extracted and distilled from *NIST SP 800-144 Guidelines on Security and Privacy in Public Cloud Computing*.

To maximize effectiveness and minimize costs, security must be built in from the start. Attempting to address security after implementation and deployment will prove to be more difficult and expensive.

Security details for public cloud providers are normally contained within non-negotiable service agreements. The agreements define the terms of service that are prescribed by the cloud providers. Similar to traditional information technology outsourcing contracts used by agencies, negotiated agreements can address an organization's concerns about security and privacy details. These details include vetting of employees, data ownership, isolation of tenant applications, data encryption and segregation, tracking and reporting service effectiveness, compliance with laws and regulations, and the use of validated products meeting federal or national standards (e.g., *Federal Information Processing Standard 140*).

Critical data and applications may require an agency to undertake a negotiated service agreement to use a public cloud. Points of negotiation can negatively affect the economies of scale that a non-negotiable service agreement brings to public cloud computing. As an alternative, the organization may be able to work around identified shortcomings in the public cloud service. Other alternatives include using a private cloud, which offers greater oversight and control of security.

Figure 15 illustrates the differences in scope and control between the cloud subscriber and cloud provider. Five conceptual layers of a generalized cloud environment are identified in the diagram and apply to public clouds, as well as each of the other deployment models.

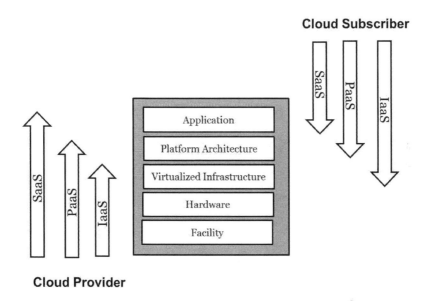

Figure 15 Differences in Scope and Control among Cloud Service Models[7]

The arrows at the left and right of the diagram denote the approximate range of control for a cloud provider and user. In general, the higher the level of support from a cloud provider, the less control the cloud subscriber has over the system.

The two lowest layers denote the physical elements of a cloud environment, which are under the full control of the cloud provider. These include heating, ventilation, air conditioning (HVAC), power,

---

[7] Reprinted courtesy of the National Institute of Standards and Technology, U.S. Department of Commerce. Not copyrightable in the United States. https://downloads.cloudsecurityalliance.org/initiatives/guidance/NIST-Draft-SP-800-144_cloud-computing.pdf

communications, etc. The remaining layers denote the logical elements of a cloud environment. The virtualized infrastructure layer entails hypervisors, VMs, virtual data storage, and supporting middleware components.

Similarly, the platform architecture layer entails compilers, libraries, utilities, and other software tools needed to implement applications. The application layer represents deployed software applications made available via the cloud.

Although reducing cost and increasing efficiency are primary motivations for moving towards a public cloud, reducing responsibility for security should not be. Ultimately, the organization is accountable for the overall security of the outsourced cloud service. Monitoring and addressing security issues that arise remain in the purview of the organization, as does oversight over other important issues such as performance and availability. Because cloud computing brings with it new security challenges, it is essential for an organization to oversee and manage how the cloud provider secures and maintains the computing environment.

The Security Upside

While the biggest obstacle facing public cloud computing is security, the cloud computing paradigm provides opportunities for innovation in provisioning security services that improve the overall security. The biggest beneficiaries are likely to be smaller organizations that have limited numbers of IT administrators and security personnel, and lack the economies of scale available to larger organizations.

The following subsections describes the potential areas of improvement where organizations can derive security benefits from transitioning to a public cloud computing environment.

Staff Specialization

Cloud providers typically have staff specializing in security, systems engineering, and networking. Through increased specialization, there is an opportunity for staff members to gain in-depth experience, take remedial actions, and make security improvements more readily than otherwise would be possible with a diverse set of duties.

Platform Strength

The structure of cloud computing platforms is typically more uniform and homogeneous. Cyber security response activities profit from a uniform, homogeneous cloud infrastructure, as do systems management, fault management, load balancing, and maintenance.

Resource Availability

The scalability of cloud computing facilities allows for greater availability. Redundancy and disaster recovery capabilities are built into cloud computing environments, and on-demand resource capacity can be used for better resilience.

Backup and Recovery

The backup and recovery policies and procedures of a cloud service may be superior to those of the organization. If copies are maintained in diverse geographic locations, these policies and procedures may be more robust. Data maintained within a cloud can be more available, faster to restore, and more reliable in many circumstances than when it is maintained in a traditional data center. Under such conditions, cloud services could also serve as a means for offsite backup storage in lieu of using traditional tape-based offsite storage.

Mobile Endpoints

The architecture of a cloud solution extends to the client at the service endpoint used to access hosted applications. Cloud clients can be either browser-based or applications-based. Since the main computational resources needed are held by the cloud provider, clients are generally lightweight computationally and easily supported on laptops, notebooks, and netbooks, as well as embedded devices such as smart phones, tablets, and personal digital assistants.

Data Concentration

Data maintained and processed in the cloud can present less of a risk to an organization with a mobile workforce than having that data dispersed on portable computers or removable media out in the field, where theft and loss of devices routinely occur. Many organizations have already made the transition to support access to organizational data from mobile devices to improve workflow management and gain other operational efficiencies.

Besides providing a computing platform or substitute for in-house applications, the public cloud services described in the following subsections can also be focused on provisioning security to other computing environments.

Data Center Oriented

Cloud services can be used to improve the security of data centers. For example, electronic mail can be redirected to a cloud provider via Mail Exchange (MX) records, examined and analyzed collectively with similar transactions from other data centers to discover widespread spam, phishing, and malware campaigns, and used to carry out a remedial action (e.g., quarantining suspect messages and content) more comprehensively than a single organization would be able to do.

Cloud Oriented

Cloud services are available to improve the security of other cloud environments. For example, reverse proxy products are available that enable unfettered access to a SaaS environment, yet maintain the data stored in that environment in encrypted form. Cloud-based identity management services also exist, which can be used to augment or replace an organization's directory service for identification and authentication of cloud users.

The Security Downside

Besides its many potential benefits for security and privacy, public cloud computing also brings with it potential areas of concern when compared with computing environments found in traditional data centers. Some of the more fundamental concerns include the information in the following subsections.

System Complexity

A public cloud computing environment is extremely complex compared with that of a traditional data center. Many components comprise a public cloud, resulting in a large attack surface. Besides components for general computing (such as deployed applications,

VM monitors, guest VMs, data storage, and supporting middleware), there are also components that comprise the management backplane (such as those for self-service, resource metering, quota management, data replication and recovery, etc.).

Security depends not only on the correctness and effectiveness of many components, but also on the interactions among them. The number of possible interactions between components increases as the square of the number of components, which pushes the level of complexity upward. The more complex as system is, the more challenging it is to secure.

Shared Multi-Tenant Environment

Subscribing organizations share components and resources with other subscribers. Having to share an infrastructure with unknown outside parties can be a drawback for some applications, and requires a high level of assurance for the strength of the security mechanisms used for logical separation.

Internet-Facing Services

Public cloud services are delivered over the Internet, exposing administrative interfaces that are used to self-service an account. Applications and data that were previously accessed from the confines of an organization's intranet must now face increased risk from network threats that were previously defended against at the perimeter of the organization's intranet.

Loss of Control

Migrating to a public cloud requires a transfer of control to the cloud provider over information, as well as system components that were previously under the organization's direct control. Loss of control over both the physical and logical aspects of the system may or may not provide better security (depends on the capabilities of your organization).

Dealing with cloud services requires attention to the roles and responsibilities involved, particularly with respect to managing risks. Ensuring that systems are secure and risk is managed is the responsibility of both the CSP and cloud subscriber.

Audit mechanisms and tools should be in place to determine how data is stored, protected, and used to validate services and verify policy enforcement. A risk management program should also be in place that is flexible enough to deal with the continuously-evolving and shifting risk landscape.

Information Security Laws and Regulations

The federal government must abide by certain security laws and regulations. The Clinger-Cohen Act assigns responsibilities for the efficiency, security, and privacy of computer systems within the federal government. This Act also establishes a comprehensive approach for executive agencies to improve the acquisition and management of their information resources.

The Privacy Act of 1974 likewise governs the collection, maintenance, use, and dissemination of personally-identifiable information about individuals that is maintained in the system records by federal agencies. The Federal Information Security Management Act (FISMA) requires federal agencies to adequately protect their data and information systems against unauthorized access, use, disclosure, disruption, modification, or destruction.

Federal Information Security Management Act (FISMA)[8]

FISMA mandates protecting information systems used or operated by an agency, a contractor of an agency, or other organization on behalf of an agency. That is, any external provider handling federal information or operating information systems on behalf of the federal government must meet the same security requirements as the source federal agency. The security requirements also apply to external subsystems storing, processing, or transmitting federal information and any services provided by or associated with the subsystem.

Risk Management Framework (RMF)[9]

The risk-based approach to security control selection and specification considers effectiveness, efficiency, and constraints due to applicable laws, directives, Executive Orders, policies, standards, or regulations. This section describes the activities related to managing organizational risk that are paramount to an effective information security program. Risk Management Framework (RMF) can be applied to both new and legacy information systems within the context of the system development lifecycle and the Federal Enterprise Architecture.

Step 1: Categorize

Categorize the information system and information processed, stored, and transmitted by that system based on an impact analysis.

---

[8] Reprinted courtesy of the National Institute of Standards and Technology, U.S. Department of Commerce. Not copyrightable in the United States. http://nvlpubs.nist.gov/nistpubs/SpecialPublications/NIST.SP.800-53Ar4.pdf

[9] Reprinted courtesy of the National Institute of Standards and Technology, U.S. Department of Commerce. Not copyrightable in the United States. http://csrc.nist.gov/groups/SMA/fisma/framework.html

Step 2: Select

Select an initial set of baseline security controls for the information system based on the security categorization. Tailor and supplement the security control baseline as needed based on the organization assessment of risk and local conditions.

Step 3: Implement

Implement the security controls and document how the controls are deployed within the information system and environment of operation.

Step 4: Assess

Assess the security controls using appropriate procedures to determine the extent to which the controls are implemented correctly, operating as intended, and producing the desired outcome with respect to meeting the security requirements for the system.

Step 5: Authorize

Authorize the information system operation based upon a determination of the risk to organizational operations and assets, individuals, other organizations, and the nation resulting from the operation of the information system and decision that this risk is acceptable.

Step 6: Monitor

Monitor and assess selected security controls in the information system on an ongoing basis, including assessing security control effectiveness, documenting changes to the system or environment of operation, conducting security impact analyses of the associated changes, and reporting the security state of the system to appropriate organizational officials. The following figure illustrates the steps of the NIST RMF.

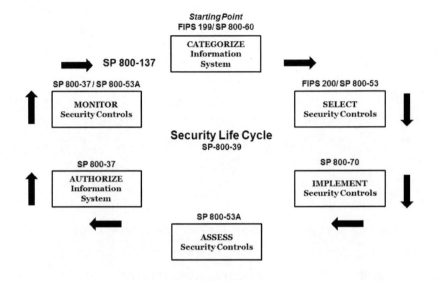

Figure 16 NIST RMF

NIST *Special Publication 800-53* defines the security controls that should be applied to an IT enterprise. A security control is a safeguard or countermeasure that removes or minimizes the security risks. NIST's *Assessing Security and Privacy Controls in Federal Information Systems and Organizations, Special Publication 800-53A* is written to facilitate security control assessments and privacy control assessments conducted within an effective risk management framework. The control assessment results provide organizational officials with:

- Evidence about the effectiveness of implemented controls.
- An indication of the quality of the risk management processes employed within the organization.

- Information about the strengths and weaknesses of information systems that are supporting organizational missions and business functions in a global environment of sophisticated and changing threats.

The findings produced by assessors are used to determine the overall effectiveness of security and privacy controls associated with information systems (including system-specific, common, and hybrid controls) and their environments of operation, and provide credible and meaningful inputs to the organization's risk management process. A well-executed assessment helps to:

- Determine the validity of the controls contained in the organization's security plans and privacy plans, and are subsequently employed in organizational information systems and environments of operation.
- Facilitate a cost-effective approach to correcting weaknesses or deficiencies in systems in an orderly and disciplined manner consistent with organizational mission/business needs.

Special Publication 800-53A is a companion guideline to *Security and Privacy Controls for Federal Information Systems and Organizations, Special Publication 800-53*. Each publication provides guidance for implementing specific steps in the RMF . *Special Publication 800-53* covers Step 2 in the RMF, and security and privacy control selection (i.e., determining which controls are needed to manage risks to organizational operations and assets, individuals, other organizations, and the nation). *Special Publication 800-53A* covers RMF Step 4 of Assess and Step 6 of Monitor, and provides guidance on the security assessment and privacy assessment processes. This guidance includes how to build effective assessment plans and analyze and manage assessment results.

Special Publication 800-53A allows organizations to tailor the basic assessment procedures provided. The concepts of tailoring used in this document are similar to the concepts described in *Special Publication 800-53*. Tailoring involves customizing the assessment procedures to more closely match the characteristics of the information system and its environment of operation. The tailoring process gives organizations the flexibility needed to avoid assessment approaches that are unnecessarily complex or costly, while simultaneously meeting the assessment requirements established by applying the fundamental concepts in the RMF. Tailoring can also include adding assessment procedures or assessment details to adequately meet the risk management needs of the organization (e.g., adding system/platform-specific information for selected controls).

Tailoring decisions are left to the discretion of the organization to maximize the flexibility in developing assessment plans—applying the results of risk assessments to determine the extent, rigor, and level of intensity of the assessments. While flexibility continues to be an important factor in developing security assessment plans and privacy assessment plans, consistency of assessments is also an important consideration. A major design objective for *Special Publication 800-53A* is to provide an assessment framework and initial starting point for assessment procedures that are essential for achieving such consistency.

Other government and industry-association requirements, such as the Health Insurance Portability and Accountability Act (HIPAA) and the Payment Card Industry Data Security Standard (PCI DSS), may apply to a particular organization. For example, the Veterans Health Administration (VHA) falls under HIPAA standards for private and public health care facilities, and applies to both employees and contractors. HIPAA requires both technical and physical safeguards for controlling access to data, which may create compliance issues for some cloud providers. Cloud providers are becoming more sensitive to legal and regulatory concerns, and may be willing to commit to store and process data in specific jurisdictions and apply required safeguards for security and privacy. However, the degree to which they will accept liability for exposure of content under their control remains to be seen. Even so, organizations are ultimately accountable for the security and privacy of data held by a cloud provider on their behalf.

Federal Risk and Authorization Management Program (FedRAMP)

The Federal Risk and Authorization Management Program (FedRAMP) is a government-wide program that provides a standardized approach to security assessment, authorization, and continuous monitoring for cloud products and services. FedRAMP streamlines federal agencies' abilities to make use of CSP platforms and offerings. FedRAMP is used by the government when conducting risk assessments, security authorizations, and granting ATOs for all agency use of cloud services. One of the major benefits of FedRAMP is that it allows for federal agencies to save significant time, costs, and resources since security controls from FedRAMP can be inherited by other agencies as part of their security Authorization and Approval (A&A) package.

The CSP is responsible for implementing FedRAMP security controls, hiring an independent third-party assessor organization (3PAO) to perform initial and annual assessments, creating and maintaining its authorization, and complying with continuous monitoring requirements.

Within the FedRAMP Concept of Operations (CONOPS), once an authorization has been granted, the CSP's security posture is monitored according to the assessment and authorization process. To receive reauthorization of a FedRAMP Provisional Authorization from year-to-year, CSPs must demonstrate that the security posture of their service offering is continuously acceptable.

Trust

Under the cloud computing paradigm, an organization relinquishes direct control over many aspects of security and, in doing so, confers a level of trust onto the cloud provider.

Insider Access

Data processed or stored outside the confines of an organization, its firewall, and other security controls, bring with it an inherent level of risk. The insider security threat is a well-known issue for most organizations and, despite the name, applies as well to outsourced cloud services. Insider threats go beyond those posed by current or former employees to include contractors, organizational affiliates, and other parties that have received access to an organization's networks, systems, and data to carry out or facilitate operations. Incidents may involve various types of fraud, sabotage of information resources, and theft of confidential information. Incidents may also be caused unintentionally. Moving data and applications to a cloud computing environment operated by a cloud provider still presents some level of risk for insider threats.

Data Ownership

The organization's ownership rights over the data must be firmly established in the service contract to enable a basis for trust. Ideally, the contract should state clearly that the organization retains ownership over all its data and that the cloud provider:

- Does not acquire rights or licenses through the agreement to use the data for its own purposes, including intellectual property rights or licenses.
- Does not acquire and may not claim any security interest in the data. For these provisions to work as intended, the terms of data ownership must not be subject to unilateral amendment by the cloud provider.

Visibility

Migration to public cloud services relinquishes some of the control to the cloud provider for securing the systems on which the organization's data and applications operate. Management, procedural, and technical controls used in the cloud must be commensurate with those used for internal organizational systems or surpass them, to avoid creating gaps in security. Cloud providers are typically reluctant to provide all the details of their security and privacy, since such information might be used to devise an avenue of attack.

Risk Management

With cloud-based services, some subsystems or subsystem components are outside of the direct control of a subscribing organization. Risk management is the process of identifying and assessing risk, and taking the necessary steps to reduce it to an acceptable level. Public cloud-based systems, as with traditional information systems, require that risks are managed throughout the system lifecycle. Assessing and managing risk in systems that use cloud services can be a challenge. To the extent practical, the organization should ensure that security controls are implemented correctly, operate as intended, and meet its security requirements.

Attack Surface

The hypervisor or VM monitor is an additional layer of software between an OS and a hardware platform that is used to operate multi-tenant VMs. Besides virtualized resources, the hypervisor normally supports other application programming interfaces to conduct administrative operations, such as launching, migrating, and terminating VM instances. Compared with a traditional non-virtualized implementation, the addition of a hypervisor causes an increase in the attack surface.

The increased availability and use of social media, personal webmail, and other publicly available sites also have associated risks that are a concern, since they can negatively impact the security of the browser, its underlying platform, and cloud services accessed through social engineering attacks. As part of the overall security architecture for cloud computing, organizations need to review existing measures and employ additional ones, if necessary, to secure the client side.

Server-Side Protection

Much like their non-virtual counterparts, virtual servers and applications need to be secured in IaaS clouds, both physically and logically. Following organizational policies and procedures, hardening of the OS and applications should occur to produce VM images for deployment. Virtual firewalls can be used to isolate groups of VMs from other hosted groups, such as production systems from development systems or development systems from other cloud-resident systems. Carefully managing VM images is also important to avoid accidentally deploying images under development or containing vulnerabilities. A hybrid cloud is a type of composite cloud with similar protection issues. In a hybrid cloud, the infrastructure consists of a private cloud composed with either a public cloud or another organization's private cloud. The clouds themselves remain unique entities, bound together by standardized or proprietary technology that enables unified service delivery, but also creates interdependency. For example, identification and authentication might be performed through an organization's private cloud infrastructure as a means for its users to gain access to services provisioned in a public cloud.

Identity and Access Management (IAM)

Data sensitivity and privacy of information have become increasingly an area of concern for organizations, and unauthorized access to information resources in the cloud is a major concern. One recurring issue is that the organizational identification and authentication framework may not naturally extend into the cloud, and extending or changing the existing framework to support cloud services may be challenging. The alternative of employing two different authentication systems, one for the internal organizational systems and another for external cloud-based systems, is a complication that needs to be addressed. Identity federation, popularized with the introduction of service oriented architectures, is one solution that can be accomplished in a number of ways, such as with the Security Assertion Markup Language (SAML) standard or the OpenID standard.

The following figure illustrates how SAML works.

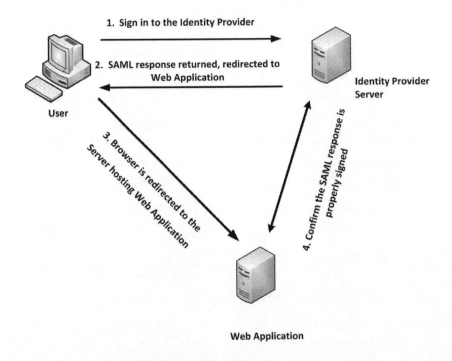

Figure 17 SAML Operation Flow

1. The user signs into the identity provider with his/her credentials, and selects an application to access.
2. The identity provider returns a digitally-signed SAML response.
3. The browser is redirected to the server hosting the web application.
4. The server confirms that the SAML response is properly signed, and allows access to the web application.

SAML is a secure and scalable security method for organizations that need access to a variety of resources across the internet.

Authentication

A growing number of cloud providers support the SAML standard, and use it to administer users and authenticate them before providing access to applications and data. SAML provides a means to exchange information, such as assertions related to a subject or authentication information, between cooperating domains.

SAML request and response messages are typically mapped over the Simple Object Access Protocol (SOAP), which relies on the eXtensible Markup Language (XML) for its format. SOAP messages are digitally signed. For example, once a user has established a public key certificate for a public cloud, the private key can be used to sign SOAP requests. SOAP message security validation is complicated and must be carried out carefully to prevent attacks. There is an attack technique called XML wrapping that involves manipulating SOAP messages.

A new element (i.e., the wrapper) is introduced into the SOAP Security header, and then the original message body is moved under the wrapper and replaced by a bogus body containing an operation defined by the attacker. The original body can still be referenced and its signature verified, but the operation in the replacement body is executed instead.

Access Control

SAML alone is not sufficient to provide cloud-based Identity and Access Management (IAM) services. The capability to adapt cloud subscriber privileges and maintain control over access to resources is also needed. As part of identity management, standards like the eXtensible Access Control Markup Language (XACML) can be used by a cloud provider to control access to cloud resources, instead of using a proprietary interface. XACML focuses on the mechanism for arriving at authorization decisions, which complements SAML's focus on the means for transferring authentication and authorization decisions between cooperating entities. XACML is capable of controlling the proprietary service interfaces of most providers, and some cloud providers already have it in place.

Software Isolation

High degrees of multi-tenancy over large numbers of platforms are needed for cloud computing to achieve the envisioned flexibility of on-demand provisioning of reliable services, and the cost benefits and efficiencies due to economies of scale. To reach the desired high scales of consumption, cloud providers have to ensure dynamic flexible delivery of service and isolation of subscriber resources. It is important to note that applications deployed on guest VMs remain susceptible to attack and compromise, much the same as their non-virtualized counterparts.

Data Protection

Data stored in the cloud typically resides in a shared environment collocated with data from other customers. Organizations moving sensitive and regulated data into the cloud, therefore, must account for the means by which access to the data is controlled and kept secure.

Data Isolation

Data can take many forms. For example, for cloud-based application development, data includes the application programs, scripts, and configuration settings, along with the development tools. For deployed applications, data includes records and other content created or used by the applications, as well as account information about the users of the applications. Access controls are one means to keep data away from unauthorized users, and encryption is another.

Access controls are typically identity-based, which make authentication of the user's identity an important issue in cloud computing. Database environments used in cloud computing can vary significantly. For example, some environments support a multi-instance model, while others support a multi-tenant model. The former provides a unique database management system running on a VM instance for each cloud subscriber, giving the subscriber complete control over role definition, user authorization, and other administrative tasks related to security.

The latter provide a predefined environment for the cloud subscriber that is shared with other tenants, typically through tagging data with a subscriber identifier. Tagging gives the appearance of exclusive use of the instance, but relies on the cloud provider to establish and maintain a sound secure database environment. For example, certain features like data encryption are only viable with arrangements that use separate rather than shared databases. These sorts of tradeoffs require careful evaluation of the suitability of the data management solution for the data involved. Requirements in certain fields, such as healthcare, would likely influence the choice of database and data organization used in an application.

Data must be secured while at rest, in transit, and in use, and access to the data must be controlled. Standards for communications protocols and public key certificates allow data transfers to be protected using cryptography. Currently, the responsibility for cryptographic key management falls mainly on the cloud service subscriber.

Key generation and storage is usually performed outside the cloud using hardware security modules, which do not scale well to the cloud paradigm. NIST's Cryptographic Key Management Project is identifying scalable and usable cryptographic key management and exchange strategies for use by government, which could eventually help to alleviate the problem.

Data Sanitization

The data sanitization practices that a cloud provider implements have obvious implications for security. Sanitization is the removal of sensitive data from a storage device in various situations, such as when a storage device is removed from service or moved elsewhere to be stored. Data sanitization also applies to backup copies made for recovery and restoration of service, and also residual data remaining upon termination of service.

Availability

In simple terms, availability is the extent to which an organization's full set of computational resources is accessible and usable. Availability can be affected temporarily or permanently, and a loss can be partial or complete. Denial of Service (DoS) attacks, equipment outages, and natural disasters are all threats to availability. The concern is that most downtime is unplanned and can impact the mission of the organization.

Temporary Outages

Despite employing architectures designed for high-service reliability and availability, cloud computing services can and do experience outages and performance. Periods of scheduled maintenance are also usually excluded as a source of downtime in Service Level Agreements (SLAs), and are able to be scheduled by the cloud provider with short notice. The level of reliability of a cloud service and its capabilities for backup and recovery need to be addressed in the organization's contingency.

Denial of Service (DoS)

A DoS attack involves saturating the target with bogus requests to prevent it from responding to legitimate requests in a timely manner. An attacker typically uses multiple computers or a botnet to launch an assault. Even an unsuccessful distributed DoS attack can quickly consume large amounts of resources to defend against and cause charges to soar.

Value Concentration

A response to the question, "Why do you rob banks?" is often attributed to Willie Sutton, a historic and prolific bank robber who answered, "because that is where the money is."[10] In many ways, data records are the currency of the 21st century and cloud-based data stores are the bank vault, making them an increasingly preferred target.

When asked why he robbed banks, Sutton simply replied,

"Because that's where the money is."

Figure 18 Bank Robber Willie Sutton

---

[10] Reprinted courtesy of the FBI. Not copyrightable in the United States. http://www.fbi.gov/about-us/history/famous-cases/willie-sutton

Incident Response

As the name implies, incident response involves an organized method for dealing with the consequences of an attack against the security of a computer system. The cloud provider's role is vital in performing incident response activities, including incident verification, attack analysis, containment, data collection and preservation, problem remediation, and service restoration.

Revising an organization's incident response plan to address differences between the organizational computing environment and a cloud computing environment is an important, but easy-to-overlook prerequisite to transitioning applications and data. Collaboration between the service subscriber and provider in recognizing and responding to an incident is essential to security and privacy in cloud computing. The complexity of the service can obscure recognition and analysis of incidents.

Understanding and negotiating the provisions and procedures for incident response should be done before entering a service contract, rather than as an afterthought. The geographic location of data is a related issue that can impede an investigation, and is a relevant subject for contract discussions. Response to an incident should be handled in a way that limits damage and reduces recovery time and costs. Being able to convene a mixed team of representatives from the cloud provider and service subscriber quickly is an important facet to meeting this goal. Remedies may involve only a single party or require the participation of both parties.

Resolution of a problem may also affect other subscribers of the cloud service. It is important that cloud providers have a transparent response process and mechanisms to share information with their subscribers during and after the incident.

Attackers

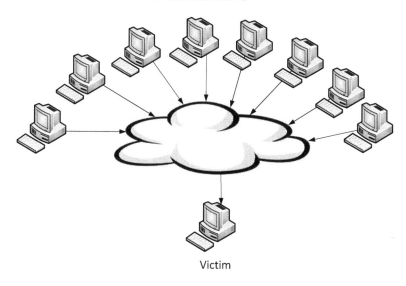

Victim

Figure 19 DoS Attack

Specify Requirements

The organization should identify its security, privacy, and other requirements for CSPs. Common security requirements include the following items:

- Personnel requirements, including clearances and responsibilities
- Access control
- Service availability
- Problem reporting, review, and resolution
- Information handling and disclosure agreements and procedures
- Physical and logical access controls
- Network connectivity and filtering
- Configuration and patch management
- Backup and recovery

71

- Incident reporting, handling, and response
- Continuity of operations
- Account and resource management
- Certification and accreditation
- Assurance levels
- Independent auditing of services.

Other requirements related to security, such as privacy, data ownership rights, records management controls, and user training should also be identified.

Assess the Competency of the Cloud Provider

Before the contract for outsourced services is awarded, the organization should evaluate the cloud provider's ability and commitment to deliver the services over the target timeframe and meet the security and privacy levels stipulated. Interviewing current subscribers of the cloud provider and assessing their level of satisfaction can also provide insight into the competency of the cloud provider. Evaluating the privacy and security levels of the services should be done thoroughly, including consideration of the following items[12]:

- Experience and technical expertise of personnel
- Vetting process that personnel undergo
- Quality and frequency of security and awareness training provided to personnel
- Type and effectiveness of the security services provided and underlying mechanisms used
- Adoption rate of new technologies
- Cloud provider's track record and ability to meet the organization's security and privacy policy, procedures, and regulatory compliance needs.

Summary

Cloud computing promises to have far-reaching effects on the systems and networks of federal agencies and other organizations. Many of the features that make cloud computing attractive can also be at odds with traditional security models and controls. Determining the security of complex computer systems composed together is also a long-standing security issue that plagues large-scale computing in general, and cloud computing in particular. Nevertheless, public cloud computing is a compelling computing paradigm that agencies need to incorporate as part their information technology solution set.

Accountability for security and privacy in public clouds remains with the organization. Federal agencies and companies must ensure that any selected public cloud computing solution is configured, deployed, and managed to meet the security, privacy, and other requirements of the organization. Organizational data must be protected in a manner consistent with policies, whether in the organization's computing center or the cloud. The organization must ensure that security and privacy controls are implemented correctly and operate as intended.

The transition to an outsourced, public cloud computing environment is in many ways an exercise in risk management. Risk management entails identifying and assessing risk, and taking the steps to reduce it to an acceptable level. Throughout the system lifecycle, risks that are identified must be carefully balanced against the security and privacy controls available and the expected benefits from their utilization. Federal agencies and organizations should work to ensure an appropriate balance between the number and strength of controls and the risks associated with cloud computing solutions.

4. The 4 D's© Migration Methodology

Cloud Migration Methodology

Migrating to the cloud is more difficult than most people think. A typical IT environment is complex, with a portfolio of hundreds of applications created independently based on different design standards created by different engineers at different times and in different situations. The applications were most likely designed with different engineering standards and design philosophies. There are very specific server, network, storage, and security configurations that need to be made. Also, each application is different and may contain complex integration points with other applications or databases.

In addition, legacy applications were never designed for the cloud. Some are tied to outdated OSs, drivers, or specialized hardware. They may also have certain assumptions as to what the latency, throughput, scalability, and access rights are within an environment. This means they do not work without some sort of modification or changes to their configuration.

Migration Decisions

Moving applications to the cloud requires designing for the cloud. When deciding whether or not to migrate existing functionality to the cloud, the decision criteria are more complex than for new builds. Key questions in "cloud planning" include:

- Should I migrate to a public cloud (and if so, which one), or a private cloud within my existing data center?
- How can I tell if my application can be moved to the public cloud at all?

- Should I hybridize my application to move some part of functionality to the public cloud while keeping other components on an internal private cloud?
- When should I consider public cloud SaaS solutions for my end users?

With these questions and challenges, a sound and proven cloud migration methodology must be followed to be successful. Many consultants or contractors will tell you that they follow "best practices" for cloud design and migration. If their custom methodology does not even have a name, then it probably doesn't exist. This brings us to my first rule (I call these rules "Ray Rules" throughout the book) of:

> If someone says they follow best practices, it usually means they don't have any.

To be successful, you need a documented methodology that provides repeatable proven processes. If your team or contractor does not have a methodology, then you are free to use the 4 D's methodology defined in this book. The basic steps are shown in the following figure.

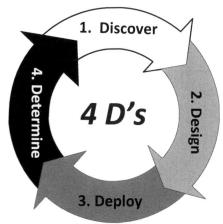

Figure 20 The 4 D's Migration Methodology

75

Discover Phase

The first step in planning a move to the cloud is knowing what you have in your IT environment. This should be an easy task since everyone has accurate and current documentation of their IT enterprise, right? Not a chance. In 20 years of consulting, I have yet to find an organization that has documentation that is sufficient for a data center move or cloud migration. The documentation is either outdated or not detailed enough to be of any use.

To complicate things, large organizations usually have multiple "stove-piped" groups delivering IT services (Service Desk, Network Engineering, Database Engineering, System Administrators, etc.). This means the responsibility for creating and approving IT enterprise documentation will be distributed among the groups. The levels of detail, quality, and formats will most likely vary. Even in small-to-midsize organizations where the documentation task is centralized, finding accurate detailed documentation sufficient for cloud migrations will be a stretch since the IT architecture and configurations are always changing.

To properly prepare for the cloud migration, collect and review the existing documentation and update it with the results of a comprehensive discovery effort. Discovery is the process of re-learning what is actually installed and configured in your network. The fastest way to do this is to use software tools that can learn the topology, connectivity, and application dependency in your enterprise environment. The data needs to be collected, organized, mined, and assessed for completeness. The objective is to create a comprehensive set of documentation that can be relied on for planning.

There are two basic types of discovery methods, passive and active discovery.

Passive Discovery

Passive techniques employ the use of software tools or probes to listen to traffic on network segments. The software collects traffic and examines packet header information (and sometimes the payload) for host addresses and Transmission Control Protocol (TCP) port information. The application types can be derived from the TCP port numbers contained in the packet headers.

The following figure shows a TCP/Internet Protocol (IP) packet and the location of this information.

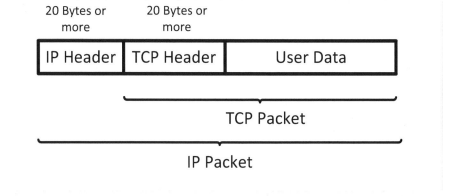

Figure 21 TCP Packet

Table 5 shows a small subset of TCP port numbers and their corresponding specific applications. Remote Network MONitoring (RMON) probes, Sniffers, or other data capture appliances can be connected to a "mirrored" interface (sometimes called Switched Port ANalyzer (SPAN) port) on a switch/router. A mirrored interface is an interface that receives traffic that is copied from one or more of the other router/switch interfaces.

This provides a central point to collect all the traffic that is coming and going on the router/switch network interfaces.

Note: If properly configured, traffic mirroring does not impact the switching performance of traffic on the interfaces.

Remember, because passive discovery relies on hosts to communicate over the network, hosts that do not transmit or receive data are not discovered by this technique.

The following figure illustrates a probe connected to a mirrored port.

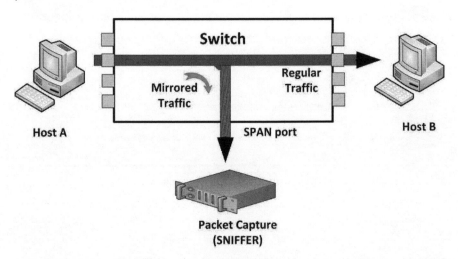

Figure 22 Mirrored Port and Sniffer Connectivity

Active Discovery

The active discovery method uses software tools that leverage Simple Network Management Protocol (SNMP), Windows Web Management Interface (WMI), and Internet Control Message Protocol (ICMP) echo requests or "pings" to remotely query routers, switches, and servers.

The SNMP discovery process finds IP-enabled network devices connected to your network. (A device is defined as any piece of equipment that has at least one physical network interface and IP address). As SNMP aware routers are found on the network, the process looks into the Management Information Base (MIB2) routing table and finds external network addresses. The discovered routers can also provide external host addresses through entries contained in their Address Resolution Protocol (ARP) tables.

The client/server applications located on the previously-discovered hosts can be obtained by scanning the host for open TCP port ranges. Many applications use standard TCP ports as shown in Table 5. You can determine applications that are installed through the identification of open ports or deep packet inspection.

Table 5 Common TCP Ports

Port Number	Protocol	Network Application Description
7	TCP, UDP	Echo protocol
20	TCP	FTP data port
21	TCP	FTP control
22	TCP, UDP	Secure Shell (SSH)
25	TCP, UDP	Simple Mail Transport Protocol (SMTP) (email)
53	TCP, UDP	Domain Name Service (DNS)
80	TCP	HTTP
88	TCP	Kerberos
161	TCP, UDP	SNMP
311	TCP	Apple server admin
308	TCP	Novastor online backup
383	TCP, UDP	HP OpenView Operating Agent
366	TCP, UDP	SMTP On Demand Mail Relay
371	TCP, UDP	Clear Case
384	TCP, UDP	Remote network server system
389	TCP, UDP	Lightweight Directory Access Protocol (LDAP)
445	TCP	Microsoft SMB file share
465	TCP	Cisco protocol

Port Number	Protocol	Network Application Description
694	TCP	Linux HA heartbeat
901	TCP	Samba Web Admin
902	TCP, UDP	VMware Server Console

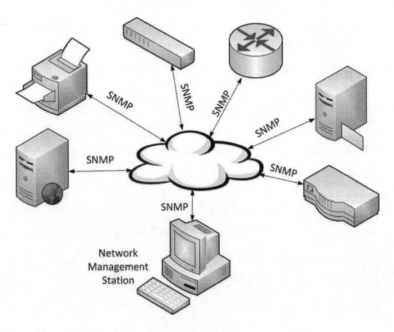

Figure 23 Discovery through SNMP Polling

Application Dependency Mapping

Learning and documenting the network topology, application locations, and connectivity is the first phase of discovery. The second and most important phase is learning and mapping out the application dependencies of your applications. An application dependency map documents the upstream and downstream application relationships.

Understanding the dependencies between your applications helps you architect a high-performance solution in the cloud as well as facilitate troubleshooting. Cloud migrations require extracting applications from their data flows and feeds. Applications and their dependent components must move together to the cloud in order for the application to work.

Mapping dependencies can also help identify performance improvement areas and identify ways to reduce costs through consolidation. There are automated tools that not only discover the network topology, application locations, and connectivity, but also the dependencies between other applications. These tools include BMC Atrium, HP Discovery and Dependency Mapping Advanced Edition (DDMA) software, and vCenter Infrastructure Navigator (VIN). The tools can auto discover the application dependency links by observing and documenting the data flow and connectivity details.

This information is required before you can determine which applications are to be moved when to the cloud. The dependencies are best viewed through application maps as shown in the following figure.

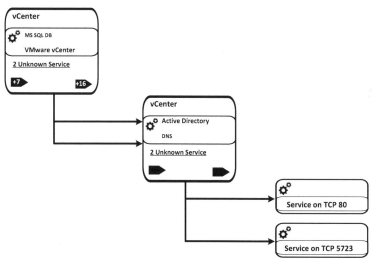

Figure 24 Dependency Mapping Illustration[11]

---

[11] Van den Berg, Viktor. Cloud Management, Server Virtualization. Web. 18 July 2013. http://www.viktorious.nl/2013/07/18/vcenter-infrastructure-navigator/

Figure 24 on the previous page shows the VMware VIN tool output that has discovered and mapped out a server named *vcenter* in the top-left corner running vCenter and MS SQL service, and connects to a server running Active Directory, DNS, and two unknown services on TCP ports 80 and 5723. The tags on the top server show that 7+ services are connecting to this VM, which is connected to 16 other services. When the tags are clicked, the mapping diagram expands to show additional application dependencies.

Once you have the application dependencies mapped, identify the ones that have the lowest number of dependencies with other applications. These applications should be migrated first since they are less complicated, and therefore, easier to migrate, test, and support.

Baselining Performance

A performance baseline is a set of performance measurements that define the typical or normal operating conditions of an enterprise infrastructure. Historical performance baselines are used for comparison purposes to detect changes that may be related to misconfigurations, hardware failures, or other problems.

The following lists a few well-known tools that can help with collecting performance and capacity information for workloads:

- SolarWinds
- Windows Performance Monitor, disk manager
- PlateSpin Recon from NetIQ (Workload analysis with remote data collection)
- VMware Capacity Planner (as a hosted service available to VMware partners, this planner collects resource utilization and compares the data against industry values)

- Cirba (utilization analysis, with normalization leveraging industry standards from SPEC.org)
- Linux (df, iostat, top, mpstat, sar)

After using discovery tools to document what you have in your IT enterprise, you need to baseline the current application performance. Baselining is necessary for several reasons. First, you need to ensure that the application performance obtained after migrating to the cloud is as good as or better than the performance obtained in the previous environment. Second, measuring end-to-end performance helps identify areas of improvement. Lastly, the performance improvements can be used as one of the elements to justify the Return on Investment (ROI) of the cloud migration (decreased application response time by x%, saved TBD$, etc.).

Although there are many performance items that can be measured, the items in the following table are the recommended minimum that should be collected for your baseline before moving to the cloud.

Table 6 Typical Baselining Metrics

Metric	Notes
CPU Utilization	<ul><li>Average</li><li>Peak</li><li>CPU Ready - per VM and per vCPU statistic, pCPU too busy/unavailable</li></ul>
Memory Utilization	<ul><li>Available free memory</li><li>Anonymous paging or thread swapping</li></ul>
Network Utilization	<ul><li>TX/RX throughput</li><li>Maximum bandwidth</li></ul>
I/O Utilization	<ul><li>Device busy %</li><li>Wait queue length</li></ul>
End-to-end Application Response Time	Time includes server and client processing time, network time, and browser rendering.
Storage Utilization	% storage space consumed.

Performance Data Metrics

To understand what the performance metric really means, it is important to understand how a value is collected and calculated.

Average and Maximum/Minimum Metrics

The average calculation provides a high-level assessment of the performance metric. We must be careful when using average values, since sample measurements that are very low or very high are "averaged out" and skew the calculation. For CPU utilization measurements, it is even more complicated as the CPU utilization measurement could be the average of *all* the CPU cores in a server. More on that later.

For now, let's look at an example where calculating the average of CPU utilization over a time period can be misleading. For example, Figure 25 on the next page illustrates a sample of CPU utilization measurements taken every 5 minutes from a Windows Server with Hyper-Threading (HT) turned off. As you can see, the average calculation tends to hide the outlier CPU measurement that peaked one time at 85% and provides an overall CPU utilization of 20.5%.

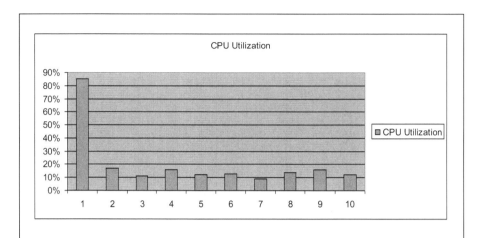

Sample Time	CPU Utilization
1.05	85%
1.1	17%
1.15	11%
1.20	16%
1.25	12%
1.30	13%
1.35	09%
1.40	14%
1.45	16%
1.50	12%

AVERAGE = (85+17+11+16+12+13+9+14+16+12)/10 samples = 20.5%

Figure 25 CPU Utilization Samples

If the 85% measurement was never recorded, the average would have been 13.3%. Because this example uses a small sample size, it is unknown if the 85% CPU measurement is an outlier that can be essentially ignored or a repeatable event that must be understood and accounted for in the cloud migration design. Therefore, metrics should be collected over a longer period of time so a larger sample size can be collected. The best time period length is a typical business cycle (or a minimum of one week).

What happens when we look at CPU utilization in real time instantaneously? You will actually see the processor either 100% or 0% utilized if you sample fast enough, because the processor is either on or off when it is working. The average CPU utilization can only be calculated by using measurements collected over a period of time. In the previous example, a CPU measurement of 85% means that the CPU was utilized 85 times out of every 100 time intervals.

How do you handle CPU utilizations in multi-CPU servers? Which CPU utilization number do you use since there is more than one? Today, servers have multiple physical CPUs, with each CPU having multiple CPU cores that can have multiple logical CPUs through the use of HT. This sounds very confusing, so let's examine what this really means.

In the "old" days, a CPU was a just a single processor chip that fit inside a single socket on a computer motherboard. Over time, manufacturers created faster CPUs by increasing the processor clock speeds, increasing the size and quantity of local cache, etc. Fast forward to today where we can now have a single CPU chip that contains multiple internal CPUs cores. Each internal core uses a feature called multi-threading, which makes each CPU *core* look like more than one processor. We call these virtual or Logical Processors (LPs).

The following provides a few definitions:

- **CPU chip**: The *physical* CPU processor that is installed on a socket located on the computer motherboard.

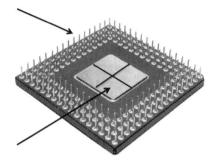

- **Processor Core**: An individual central processing unit.
- **Logical Processor**: A virtual processor that is presented through the uses of HT or multi-threading.

The following figure illustrates a single multi-core CPU with a total of 16 LPs.

Figure 26 Single Multi-Core CPU with a Total of 16 LPs

The following figure illustrates multiple CPU physical chip processors installed in 4 separate sockets within a server, providing a total of 64 logical processors.

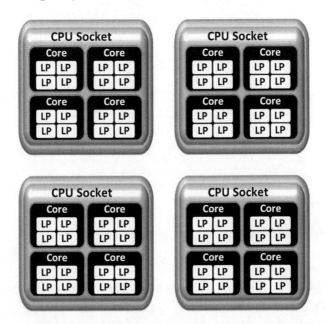

LP = Logical Processors

Figure 27 Multiple CPU Physical Processor Chips Installed in Four Separate Sockets within a Server

Simultaneous Multi-Threading (SMT) Technology

To get even more computing performance out of the processors, manufacturers have implemented a process feature called Simultaneous Multi-Threading (SMT). Multi-threading "fakes out" the OS into thinking that one physical CPU *core* appears as more than one processing unit.

Note: Intel calls their threading "hyper-threading" (HT).

We call each of these threads a virtual CPU or LP, since that is what it looks like to the OS. Multi-threading increases the number of independent instructions in the pipeline. Referring to Figure 26 on the previous page, even though the OS sees four LPs for each core, the actual CPU core only has a single processing unit. HT allows the logical CPU cores to share physical execution resources.

The physical CPU has digital logic that schedules access by the LPs, speeds up program execution, and prevent conflicts. The scheduler gives access to one LP if another LP is stalled waiting for instructions. Multi-threading is no substitute for real additional cores, but a multi-core CPU with HT can perform better than a multi-core CPU without HT.

Sar (Figure 28)[12] and Perfmon (Figure 29)[13] are software utilities provided with the Linux and Windows OSs, respectively. Perfmon provides the average CPU utilization of all the CPUs in the server. The Sar command does the same thing, unless you include **-P** within the command. The -P command tells Sar to list the CPU utilization for *all* of the processors in the server. Individual utilization for each processor is what you want. Average CPU utilization in a multi-processor environment is a totally useless metric since it can hide over-utilized processors.

[12] Bezroukov, Nikolai. Softpanorama. 5 July 2014.
http://www.softpanorama.org/Admin/Monitoring/sar.shtml
[13] Adminfoo.net. 4 April 2007. http://adminfoo.net/2007/04/windows-perfmon-top-ten-counters.html

The following figure reports CPU utilization for the 0 and 1 individual processors.

```
$ sar -u -P ALL
```

00:00:01	CPU	%user	%nice	%system	%idle
00:10:00	0	4.19	1.75	0.70	93.37
00:10:00	1	8.59	2.18	0.63	88.60
00:20:01	0	1.87	3.21	1.14	93.78
00:20:01	1	1.35	3.12	1.04	94.49
...					
23:50:01	0	42.84	0.03	0.80	56.33
23:50:01	1	45.29	0.01	0.74	53.95
Average:	0	6.00	5.01	2.74	86.25
Average:	1	5.61	4.97	2.99	86.43

NOTE:
%user – User application % utilization
%nice - % utilization for applications with a set priority level (e.g., batch jobs)
% system – System utilization %
%idle - Unused processing time

Figure 28 Example of Sar Command Output for a Dual-Core Processor (0 and 1)

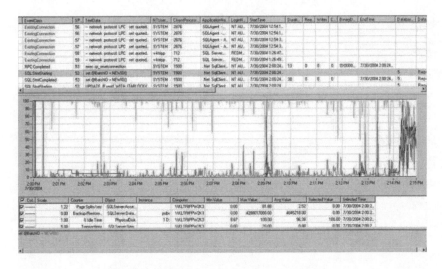

Figure 29 Example of Perfmon Output

Figure 30 illustrates the utilization of a dual-core Intel processor on a single processor chip. Because HT is off, the OS only sees the two core CPUs. Each is running at 100% utilization. Total CPU utilization calculated by Perfmon and Sar is 100%, (100+100)/2. This value makes sense since each core is saturated and working at 100%.

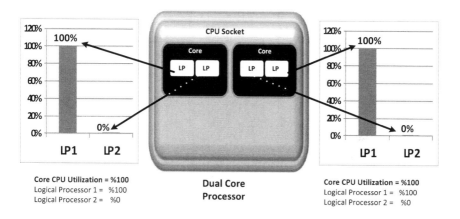

Core CPU Utilization = %100
Logical Processor 1 = %100
Logical Processor 2 = %0

**Dual Core
Processor**

Core CPU Utilization = %100
Logical Processor 1 = %100
Logical Processor 2 = %0

Figure 30 CPU Utilization of a Dual-Core Intel Processor on a Single Processor Chip

Figure 31 on the next page illustrates the same processor with HT enabled, which provides two threads or LPs per core CPU, giving a total of four LPs. The LPs are running at 81%, 19%, 73%, and 27% utilization. An average CPU utilization metric reports a utilization of 50% [81+19+73+27)/4], which is misleading and essentially wrong. Since the LPs each share a core CPU, if the LPs on a single core add up to 100%, the entire CPU core is actually at 100% utilization. So, do not rely on an average utilization metric, as you will be fooled into thinking that you are only using 50 % of your CPU—when it is actually 100%.

Why This is Important

Understanding multi-processor technology is important if you want to prevent poor performance, wasted capacity, and misleading CPU utilization reported in your cloud environment. Different cloud providers use different technology and reporting metrics, so these issues may or may not apply. The CSPs are always updating their technology, so it is up to the cloud consumer to ensure how SMT is implemented and how CPU utilization is measured.

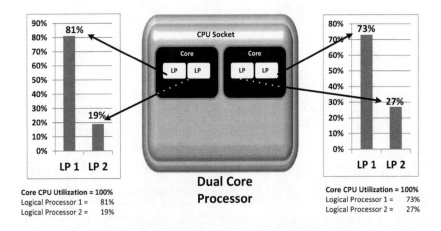

Figure 31 CPU Utilization of a Dual-Core Intel Processor on a Single Processor Chip with HT Enabled

Interpreting Minimum and Maximum Values

When viewed in relation to the average, the minimum and maximum values give valuable insight into the full spectrum of performance for a metric. Since it is important to ensure performance stays within established SLAs, we focus on the peak or maximum values.

Calculating the 95th Percentile

Since there are always outliers in any measurement, it is beneficial to sometimes toss out some of the outlying measurements. A useful calculation for this method is the 95th percentile. This calculation discards the highest 5% of the collected data samples, and the next highest remaining data sample is the "95th Percentile" value. Figure 32 Illustrates a graph of server CPU utilization collected over several weeks using SolarWinds. The figure clearly shows the average, minimum/maximum, and 95th Percentile values.

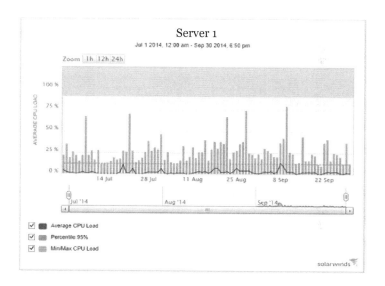

Figure 32 Server CPU Utilization Example with Average, Minimum/Maximum, and 95th Percentile Values

SNMP Polling Time Periods

Most performance metrics can be obtained through SNMP polling. For baseline purposes, the polling rate rule of thumb is every 5 minutes. If you poll much faster than that (real time or 1 minute), it is very likely that you will catch CPU utilization peaks of 100%, which are very short instantaneous usage. CPU statistics polled at 5 minutes or longer give you more meaningful trends of processor activity.

Design Phase

After discovering and documenting your applications and environment, you need to design your overall cloud environment. This design applies to IaaS and PaaS cloud based models. The design process is broken up into four (4) sections:

- ROI and Total Cost of Ownership (TCO)
- Architecture design
- Infrastructure design
- Application redesign

Return on Investment (ROI)

A business case study should be performed before moving to the cloud. Now that you have completed the Discovery phase, you should have sufficient information to create a business case as to whether it is worthwhile to move to the cloud. Even if you have already decided to migrate, determining the overall benefits from a qualitative and quantitative perspective is necessary so you can justify the migration when the project is over (people's memory of how bad and expensive the old system was tends to fade over time).

You should develop a business case that includes a strategy for leveraging the advantages of cloud computing. The advantages should show the cost savings related to shifting CAPital EXpenditures (CAPEX) to OPerational EXpenses (OPEX), as well as intangible benefits such as faster deployments, higher availability, elasticity, etc.

The standard ROI formula is expressed as:

$$ROI = \frac{(\text{Gain from Investment} - \text{Cost of Investment})}{\text{Cost of Investment}}$$

Build a Business Case

Many IT professionals use ROI and/or the TCO to build their business cases. The ROI calculation quantifies both the costs and expected benefits of moving to the cloud. TCO only compares the long-term costs of the cloud vs. the current operating environment over a specific time period.

Although many people believe that the above ROI formula is better suited for justifying a piece of hardware or software, it may not be the best measure for determining if you should invest in cloud services. Since cloud computing is a *service*, the ROI must take into account the "soft" benefits such as the value or satisfaction gained by the end users. How satisfied are the end users? This is not very easy to quantify. What are the other intangible benefits of cloud computing that should be considered? Here are a few examples of soft benefits:

- Improved application response time
- Less working capital required for the infrastructure
- Avoidance of building out to handle peak loads
- Increased customer satisfaction
- Increased employee satisfaction
- Better agility, faster time-to-market
- Risk avoidance

If the soft benefits listed above are ignored in the ROI calculation, it may be more difficult to justify the moving to the cloud.

The following two tables identify some of the hard costs that can be included in the ROI calculation.

Table 7 Current Monthly Hosting Expenses

Description	Cost	# of Months	Total
Facility Expenses (rent, power, other utilities, etc.)			
Hardware Expenses (servers, switches, routers, firewalls, etc., as well as extra hardware to handle peak loads)			
Software Licensing (applications, OSs, tools, etc., as well as extra software required to handle peak loads)			
Labor Expenses (network, system admins, DB admin, service desk, etc.)			
Internet and WAN Connectivity			
Hardware and Software Maintenance			
Other			
Intangible Benefits			
Reduction in Need for Working Capital			
Avoidance of Capacity Enhancement			
Increased Customer Satisfaction			
Increased Employee Satisfaction			
Improved Application Response Time			
Better Agility, Faster Time-to-market			

Table 8 Cloud Services Forecasted Costs/Month

Description	Cost	# of Months	Total
Processing			
Storage			
Load Balancing			
External IP Addresses			
DNS Services			
Content Delivery Services			
Network Bandwidth			
Data Transfer			
Monitoring			
Other			
Migration Related Costs			
Software Development & Integration			
Migration Downtime			
Productivity Slow Down as Users Learn New System			
Planning Labor			
Migration Labor			

Technology Refresh[14]

Agencies and businesses replace on-premise systems approximately every 5–7 years. Laptops and desktops are usually shorter with a life span of 3–5 years. When calculating the TCO, it is important to consider the upgrade costs that hit every xx number of years when it comes time to retire the old on-premise servers.

Many people fail to consider the recurring technical refresh costs when comparing cloud services to their current on-premise services. Even in situations where staying in-house may be cheaper than

---

[14] Wlodarz, Derrick. Comparing cloud vs on-premise? Six hidden costs people always forget about. March 2014. http://betanews.com/2013/11/04/comparing-cloud-vs-on-premise-six-hidden-costs-people-always-forget-about/

going to the cloud on a monthly basis, the technical refresh costs may be so hefty that it is still better migrating to the cloud in the long run.

Service Levels

Besides addressing the costs of the ROI, it should be confirmed that the service levels of the new cloud environment are equal to or better than the current service levels. The cloud SLAs should be documented in the CSP's agreement. Verify what they are and how they are calculated.

The savings in labor allows you to reassign employees originally dedicated to low-level IT tasks to more important IT project tasks. Another less-desirable option is to eliminate staff since they are no longer needed (contractors—watch out, as you are typically the first to go).

Architecture Design

The architecture should reflect the set of requirements and mission goals that your agency or company needs to accomplish. IT architecture is the fundamental underlying design of the IT *infrastructure* that supports business and mission objectives. IT architecture should align with the business/mission processes, goals, and priorities. Tightly linking the business/mission with IT offers the benefit of successful integration of systems, agility, and improved decision-making. The architecture design starts with identifying business processes/policies, mapping them to applications, and then finally mapping them to the infrastructure components.

The Open Group Architecture Framework (TOGAF) gives the purpose of defining IT architecture as, "The purpose of enterprise architecture is to optimize across the enterprise the often fragmented legacy of processes (both manual and automated) into an integrated environment that is responsive to change and supportive of the delivery of the business strategy."

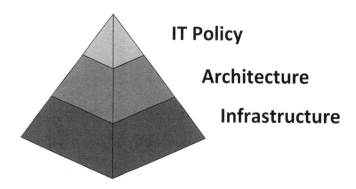

IT Policy

Architecture

Infrastructure

Figure 33 High-Level View of the Interaction of Business Processes/Policies, Architecture, and Infrastructure

The business architecture determines which assets engage in what processes to support the mission or strategy. Many competing approaches to enterprise architecture exist. Some of the most popular approaches used in government agencies and companies are:

- U.S. DoD Architecture Framework (DoDAF)
- TOGAF
- Object-oriented with Unified Modeling Language (UML)
- Zachman framework
- DYA framework
- Extended enterprise architecture framework

Architecture Models

In the simplest sense, a model is just a series of pictures and diagrams that illustrate the IT architecture. The following figure shows several views of an IT architecture.

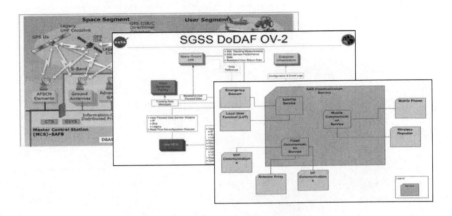

Figure 34 Example of DoDAF Views

DoDAF 2.0

The Clinger-Cohen Act dictates that the CIO must develop and maintain IT architectures within the government. For the DoD, DoDAF is used to define IT architectures. Since DoDAF is widely used throughout the DoD, we will spend some time examining this architectural framework.

DoDAF utilizes a six-step architecture development process. Unlike earlier versions of DoDAF, version 2 is data-centric rather than product-centric architecture framework, and was created to establish guidance for architecture content as a function of purpose—"fit for purpose." The data-centric approach was designed to ensure all essential data relationships are captured. The DoDAF views provide visual renderings of the underlying architectural data.

100

The following table lists all the DoDAF 2 views and describes each viewpoint's overarching aspects of architecture context that relate to all viewpoints.

Table 9 DoDAF 2 Views and Descriptions

All Viewpoint	Description
Capability Viewpoint	Articulates the capability requirements, delivery timing, and deployed capability
Data and Information Viewpoint	Articulates the data relationships and alignment structures in the architecture content for the capability and operational requirements, system engineering processes, and systems and services
Operational Viewpoint	Includes the operational scenarios, activities, and requirements that support the capabilities.
Project Viewpoint	Describes the relationships between operational and capability requirements, and the various projects being implemented. Also details the dependencies among capability and operational requirements, system engineering processes, systems design, and services design within the defense acquisition system process.
Services Viewpoint	Design for solutions articulating the performers, activities, services, and their exchanges, providing for/supporting operational and capability functions.
Standards Viewpoint	Articulates the applicable operational, business, technical, and industry policies, standards, guidance, constraints, and forecasts that apply to capability and operational requirements, system engineering processes, and systems and services.
Systems Viewpoint	For legacy support, this is the design for solutions articulating the systems, their composition, interconnectivity, and context providing for or supporting operational and capability functions.

The following figure depicts the DoDAF six-step process[15].

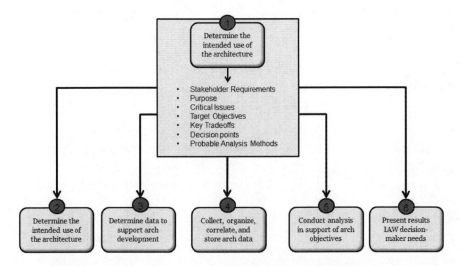

Figure 35 DoDAF 2.0 Six-Step Architecture Process DoD CIO

The following subsections provide a short summary of the six-step process.

Step 1: Determine the Intended Use of the Architecture

Document the purpose of your IT architecture. A template for collecting this information is included in the DoD Architecture Registry System (DARS). This step is not complete until you have answered questions such as:

- What is the purpose and requirements of the IT architecture?
- How will the design effort be conducted?
- What data categories are needed?

---

[15]DoD CIO.

http://dodcio.defense.gov/TodayinCIO/DoDArchitectureFramework.aspx

- What is the impact to others?
- How will you measure success?

Requirements Definition

The requirements definition requires engineers and business analysts to work very closely with the stakeholders and sponsor(s) to extract their underlying business needs. The requirement definition takes time, and I recommend avoiding the urge to rush through this process and quickly "jump into a preconceived solution." A full understanding must be captured of the mission/business, operating challenges, and basic needs of the stakeholders. Because most stakeholders do not know what they really need until they actually see it, patience is required by all through the explorative process. To ensure the best possible solution is designed, requirements should be defined in such a way that they do not dictate a particular solution. For example, an acceptable requirement might be,

> "The cloud application shall scale out horizontally to accommodate increased workloads and provide redundancy."

...but not:

> "The cloud application *shall utilize an F5 BIG-IP load balancer* to scale out horizontally and provide redundancy."

In the end, an F5 BIG-IP load balancer may be the best answer, but we do not want to bias any design considerations during the requirements definition process.

Gathering requirements is typically performed by reviewing existing documentation and interviewing stakeholders individually, in small groups, or in facilitated work sessions. The exact approach should be agreed to by the client so as to minimize any disruption of the business.

To ensure the meetings are as productive as possible, preparation and focus are extremely important. I say this because, like many of you, I have been forced to sit through some long, drawn-out, boring, and very unproductive meetings. Over the years I have learned that meetings for gathering requirements are at the top of the scale for epic meeting failures. Here are some recommended tips for hosting successful meetings for gathering requirements:

- Meetings should be scheduled at least 2 weeks ahead of time, and should include a short agenda explaining the purpose and topics of the meeting.
- The bare minimum number of attendees should be invited.
- Attendee confirmations should be verified 1 day in advance of the meeting date. Special attention should be paid to ensuring that the Subject Matter Expert(s) (SME) and key decision makers are attending the meeting—this is important because it is essential to have people who (1) understand the existing system, and (2) have the authority to make decisions at the meeting.
- To maintain focus, periodically summarize the discussion points during the meeting.
- Issues raised in the requirements review meeting that are not quickly resolved should be documented by the Project Manager and addressed later by the team (all major issues should be resolved before requirements finalization).
- All meetings should be concluded with a summary of decisions and action items.

Here is another Ray Rule as one last note on meetings:

The number of attendees in a meeting is inversely proportional to productivity, efficiency, and success.

Ensure you have just enough of the *right people* for your meetings to gather requirements—it will not be easy to meet that goal. You will find that the key people will not attend, and the people that can add no value will be lining up at the conference room door. Steve Jobs of Apple had a draconian way of ensuring the right number of people attended his meetings. In the *Insanely Simple* book by Ken Segall, the following meeting event occurred:

"In one story, Jobs was about to start a weekly meeting with Apple's ad agency.

Then Jobs spotted someone new."

"He stopped cold," Segall writes. "His eyes locked on to the one thing in the room that didn't look right. Pointing to Lorrie, he said, 'Who are you?'

Calmly, she explained that she was asked to the meeting because she was a part of related marketing projects.

Jobs heard her, and then politely told her to get out."[16]

The moral of this story is, Steve Jobs only wanted meeting attendees that had ideas to present and/or defend.

---

[16] Segall, Ken. Insanely Simple. The Obsession That Drives Apple's Success. New York Penguin Group, 2013. Print.
Also Drake, Baer "3 Ways Steve Jobs Made Meetings Insanely Productive – And Often Terrifying." Strategy. *Business Insider.* 17 December 2014. Web. 31 December 2014.

The Requirements Gathering Team should ensure that requirements associated with system quality, reliability, availability, and IT SLAs are discussed. Also, any performance improvement requirements such as faster response times, transaction volumes, number of users, etc., should be discussed and documented.

After the requirements are collected, they should be mapped out against the existing IT services to identify any gaps. Since the applications are moving to a new environment in the cloud, now is the time to design-in small changes to fill some of the less complex gaps. Some people may argue that no changes should be made to any application that is moving to the cloud since it will inject more variables and increases risk. I argue that it is okay to make some improvements, as long as they are small. The increased risk can be controlled since the applications are moved over in phases. In addition, it makes sense to quickly leverage cloud-specific benefits such as built-in load balancing, scalability, security, etc.

To aid in the requirements review process, the requirements should be listed and ranked in a Requirements Traceability Matrix (RTM). The RTM is used to identify and track requirements throughout the project lifecycle. The following table illustrates an RTM example.

Table 10 RTM Example

ID#	Description	Source	Date	Priority	Status
1	System backups must be performed daily.	Jim Welford, System Admin	4/25/15	High	Approved
1.1	Backups must be moved to tape and moved offsite weekly.	CTO	4/25/15	High	Approved
1.2	A copy of the monthly backup	Jim Welford,	7/3/15	Medium	On Hold

ID#	Description	Source	Date	Priority	Status
	tapes are shipped to the disaster recovery site.	System Admin			
2	95% of the time, the user response time for the Logistics application do not exceed 1 second.	Sally Smith, VP Shipping Services	4/25/15	High	Approved
2.1	Logistics application must be available 99.99% of the time.	CIO	9/3/15	High	Approved
2.2	Logistics application must be able to dynamically scale and support up to 100,000 users (typical simultaneous users is 21,000).	George Jeter, VP Shared Services	6/21/15	Low	Rejected
3	Logistics application server logs must be archived for up to 5 years.	CIO	9/3/15	High	Approved

The set of requirements should be ranked in terms of stakeholder priority. Some requirements will have logical dependencies and should be grouped together. For example, in Table 10 we see requirements 1.0, 1.1, and 1.2 all refer to system backups. By grouping and ranking requirements, it becomes easier to perform a tradeoff analysis and implementation phase-in scheduling. All known requirements should be captured and prioritized—even if they are beyond the current scope of the cloud migration. We need to do this because a future desired requirement may influence the current cloud design. Also, by collecting all requirements, it will be much easier to improve and expand the system in the future.

The RTM should be distributed to the stakeholders for final review. Documentation version control should be performed on all drafts and final copies of the RTM. Formal written approval of the *Requirements Specification* document should be obtained from the key stakeholders and sponsor. If you do not get written formal approval, you can count on people asking, "Who was the idiot that wanted that feature?" and "Why are we spending more time and money on those features?" This brings up my next Ray Rule:

> *The greater delay and cost linked to a failed requirement implementation, the greater senior management will claim they never heard of it or approved it.*

Step 2: Determine the Scope of Architecture

The scope defines the boundaries of the architecture, as it establishes the problem set, defines the context, and defines the proper level of detail. The clarity of scope is best determined by defining the data to be used for the architecture.

Step 3: Determine the Data Required to Support Architecture Development

In Step 2, you reviewed the type of data needed for your architecture. Now it is time to fully document the data entities, levels of detail, units of measure, and associated metadata. This is the "modeling" portion of the architecture design. This is what most people think of when they hear about "DoDAF architectures."

Step 4: Collect, Organize, Correlate, and Store Architectural Data

In this step, the data is organized, correlated, and stored in a commercial or government architecture tool such as Systems Architect, Abacus, Troux Transformation Platform, and ARIS Business Performance Edition.

Step 5: Conduct an Analyses in Support of the Architecture Objectives

Architectural data analysis determines the level of adherence to the original architecture objectives. This step also identifies the process steps and data collection requirements needed to complete the architectural design.

Step 6: Present Results in Accordance with Decision-Making Needs

This is the final step in the architecture development process and involves presenting the architectural data to varied audiences. This presentation is facilitated by the data requirements determined in Step 3, and the data collection methods employed during Step 4.

Executive Sponsorship

Executive sponsorship is a critical component of the architecture design process. Interviewing and documenting stakeholder requirements is the first step in the process as previously shown in Figure 35. Receiving constructive feedback from the stakeholders is important. Because outside participants have day jobs, most people are reluctant to spend much time contributing data and participating in analysis and business decision meetings. An executive sponsor can establish the importance of the program, which ultimately increases stakeholder participation.

Collecting Information

The architecture design should properly support the business or mission of the organization. To get the requirements right, you need to review strategic plans and objectives, as well as interview key stakeholders (senior management, business group owners, departments, end users, etc.). Know the information that you *can* get. Time is money—don't waste your time chasing down information that is unavailable or doesn't map to the strategic direction of the organization.

Another important point is to not ever assign junior people to interview and gather information from senior leaders. I have seen consulting businesses make this mistake many times. The people interviewing stakeholders quickly become the "face" of the architecture design project. Inexperienced people do not have the years of business experience and find it difficult to debate and defend why the information gathering phase is important, and why certain information must be gathered. It will doom the project before it even gets started.

Communicate

Understand the stakeholders. Not everyone has the same objective or is interested in the same metrics. The following table illustrates the key interests of important stakeholders[17].

Table 11 Key Interests of Important Stakeholders

	Increase Support to Business/Mission	Better Business/IT Alignment	Improve IT Effectiveness	Reduce IT Complexity	Reducing IT Costs
CEO	X	X	X	X	X
CIO		X	X	X	X
IT Manager			X	X	X
CFO					X
End User			X	X	

Why We Need Enterprise Architecture

Most hardware and software engineers hate architecture design, and do not see the value of spending time and money designing an enterprise architecture. Why not use the standard industry IT

---

[17] Walker, Mike. Ramblings about Industry Architecture. Web. 30 August 2017. http://blogs.msdn.com/b/mikewalker/archive/2007/08/30/obtaining-enterprise-architecture-metrics-part-1.aspx

design models and throw it all together? All you need are firewalls, DMZ, load balancers, servers, and storage. In the end, you know the engineers will just install and configure routers/switches/ firewalls, Windows, Linux, or Solaris OSs, virtualization, and whatever server hardware they normally use. So why not save time and just build it?

This is the attitude that I had early in my career. For small project designs, bypassing the architecture design step seemed to work okay. However, for larger programs, my colleagues and I quickly learned that we needed some sort of architecture design. Without it, we found ourselves trapped in constrained IT designs. After an IT system is built and operational, it is more expensive and time consuming to add functionality and security that was not properly mapped out from the start of the program.

As previously shown in Figure 35, the six-step architecture design process can be boiled down into meeting and communicating with stakeholders, documenting requirements, and then creating the architectural framework.

So what is so bad about the architecture design process? The answer to this question can be best summarized by a conversation I had years ago with an IT architect that I used to work with in which he stated, "The architecture process is a waste of time. We spend our time sitting in boring meetings with stakeholders. Half the stakeholders do not know what they want or need and the other half give us requirements that conflict with each other. More and more stakeholders don't even attend the meetings anymore except for the ones with strong opinions. Today, we spend too much time defusing arguments and fights between the remaining stakeholders. To make things worse, senior management is becoming impatient and wants to know why after several months, all we have to show for our work is some documentation and no working IT systems."

I have to admit that the IT architect's process summary was fairly accurate. Although it was painful, we actually were able to nail down and document the key, high-level requirements and the resultant framework for the enterprise architecture. We did not know it at the time, but we were practicing something called *Agile Enterprise Architecture* (Agile EA).

Agile Enterprise Architecture (EA)

Agile EA is a method for developing enterprise architectures. Instead of following the DoDAF or other architecture framework to the Nth degree, Agile EA provides simplified iterative and incremental designs. The entire process borrows from the Agile software development methodology. Agile EA is about creating architecture designs in small Increments, and creating just enough to fulfill the current task. Complete architecture designs are purposely not created. The designs evolve incrementally over time.

Remember, your architecture design needs to be just good enough to work—not perfect. The idea is that your design starts out small and is improved over time based on the feedback you receive from both the agency/business community and project teams. Agile EA helps ensure the process is effective and successful. If you do not have an effective architecture design process, then your IT design will fail to meet most of your needs, and your architects will be struggling to justify their existence.

Don't Get Too Complicated

Use a sufficient level of detail to define the architecture, and don't over complicate things. The architecture documentation must be something that someone will actually use. Figure 36 and Figure 37 are perfect illustrations of this point. Figure 37 is the famous PowerPoint slide shown to General Stanley McChrystal during the war in Afghanistan where he stated, "When we understand that slide, we'll have won the war."[18]

"When we understand that slide, we'll have won the war"

Figure 36 General Stanley McChrystal Commenting on Overly Detailed Operational View Diagram

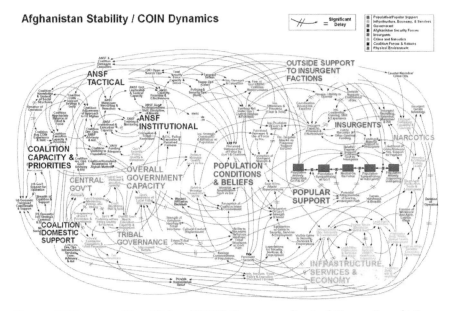

Figure 37 Famous War Slide—WTH? Overcomplicated Operational View

---

[18] Rogers, Simon. The Guardian. 29 April 2010. http://www.theguardian.com/news/datablog/2010/apr/29/mcchrystal-afghanistan-powerpoint-slide

Unlike most things in life, when it comes to documentation, bigger is not better. A document should have just enough information to get its points across, and not one word more.

Here are two more Ray Rules:

> *The thickness of a document is inversely proportional to the probability of it being read. (In other words, if it is too detailed and long, no one will ever read or use it. It will just sit on a shelf somewhere gathering dust.)*

This companion rule that is tightly coupled to Rule 1 is:

> *The probability that a customer will accept an official Program Deliverable document from a consultant is directly proportional to the thickness of the document (the inverse of Rule 1).*

The above rules are not mutually exclusive (they can both be true at the same time). Yes, customers like to get their money's worth. So you consultants out there, ensure that the first version of your deliverable document is nice and thick. You can trim down your second version to something that someone will actually read and use.

Infrastructure Design

Architecture design provides us with a good framework on which to lay our infrastructure design. This is the time that we now must complete our detailed design. From the "Discover" phase in Chapter 4, we can review our different applications and place them into groups based upon their complexity (number of dependencies) and mission criticality. The group of applications that have a low number of dependencies and low mission criticality should be migrated first to the cloud. These are the applications and workloads that are the easiest to move, operate, and support. You want to start with the easiest ones first since this provides the lowest risk of failure.

Now that you have the applications grouped and prioritized for the move, you need to decide what cloud model you will use. As previously described in the "NIST Definition of Cloud Computing" section, we need to choose SaaS, PaaS, or IaaS. Application examples for these cloud models are shown in Table 12. Once you have decided on the model for each application group, you can begin the detailed design effort.

Table 12 Application Examples for Cloud Models

Cloud Model	Application Examples
SaaS	<ul><li>Microsoft 365,</li><li>Gmail</li><li>Salesforce.com</li><li>GoToMeeting</li><li>WebEx</li></ul>
PaaS	<ul><li>Windows Azure</li><li>Amazon AWS Elastic Beanstalk</li><li>Google App Engine</li><li>Red Hat OpenShift</li><li>Heroku</li><li>Engine Yard</li></ul>
IaaS	<ul><li>Amazon AWS</li><li>Microsoft Azure</li><li>Google Compute Engine (GCE)</li></ul>

Since SaaS is fully hosted by the CSP , no infrastructure design is required by the cloud consumer. However, the cloud consumer should still perform design and risk assessments for the overall solution security, user connectivity, and access management.

Infrastructure Design within the IaaS and PaaS Cloud Models

CSPs provide all the necessary infrastructure components that are required for IaaS or PaaS deployments. The components include items such as CPU processing, memory, disk storage, network connectivity, load balancing, etc. Either you or your consulting service provider must provision and configure these components in a way that meets your overall application performance and architectural design.

Although an entire book could be written on designing a cloud infrastructure, this book discusses design tasks in general with the exception of cloud processing design. The reason for this is twofold. First, the amount and structure of cloud application processing is one of the first elements that must be completed. Second, my experience has shown that most design teams have a difficult time properly estimating the amount of processing required to properly support their applications in the cloud (for production and disaster recovery).

Calculating the Required Computing Resources

This section provides some examples of how to calculate the amount of cloud CPU processing and memory required for your application workloads. The following subsection provides examples that are specific to a private cloud VMware environment, but are also applicable to AWS, Google, or Microsoft Azure public clouds. The key concept to remember in the calculations is that we are trying to figure out the number of CPU clock cycles in Megahertz (MHz) required to process different application loads.

Let's assume that you have 100 workloads that need to be moved into the cloud and virtualized.

Assume 25% growth over 5 years.

Workload Requirement Analysis and Workload Estimations Values

Total number of CPUs = 2 CPUs

CPU per server (MHz) = 3000MHz

Average CPU utilization (percentage) = 9%

Average RAM per server (GB) = 16GB

Average RAM utilization (%) = 75%

Average Peak CPU Utilization: CPU per server (MHz) × CPU count = CPU per server (MHz)

3000MHz × 2 = 6000MHz

CPU per server (MHz) × average CPU utilization (percentage) = Workload average peak CPU utilization (MHz)

6000MHz × 9% = 540MHz

Number of workloads × Workload average peak CPU utilization (MHz) = Total peak CPU utilization (MHz)

100 × 540MHz = 54,000MHz

Therefore, we have determined that 54,000MHz is required to support 100 workloads.

---

[19]VI Kernel Blog. 26 May 2014. http://vikernel.wordpress.com/tag/calculating-the-average-peak-cpu-utilisation/

Accounting for growth:

> Total CPU (MHz) required for the VMs x (1 + % forecasted growth) = Total CPU (MHz) required
>
> 54,000MHz x (1 +.25) growth = 67,500MHz
>
> Calculating the required number of hosts to satisfy the design requirements:
>
> - Two 6-core CPU at 3000MHz per core
> - 2 sockets x 6 cores x 3000MHz = 36,000MHz per host @ 100% utilization
>
> We should never run at 100% utilization, so let's assume we'd like to have the system operating at 75% utilization. The resource utilization should be continuously monitored, since workloads do not remain static.
>
> Total host CPU in MHz x Expected CPU utilization = Total CPU utilization per ESXi host
>
> 36,000MHz x 75% = 27,000MHz
>
> Total CPU utilization per host / Total CPU utilization required = Number of hosts needed
>
> 67,500MHz / 27,000MHz = 2.5, round up to 3 hosts required.

Availability

An important design consideration for the cloud is to ensure that the system availability meets the SLAs and stakeholder expectations. Typically, availability can be increased by adding what is called N+1 redundancy. The *N* stands for the number of components (servers and VMs) necessary to run the application, and *+1* refers to the one extra backup component that takes over in the event of a failure.

The following figure is an example of designing the proper capacity for an N+1 host configuration for a VMware-based solution.

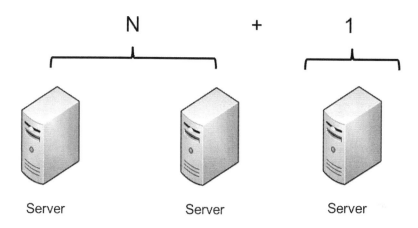

Figure 38 Illustration of N+1 Redundancy

Number of Hosts Needed for the N+1 Design Example
Calculating the average peak RAM utilization:
Average RAM per server (GB) × Average RAM utilization (Percentage) = Average peak RAM utilization (GB)
16GB × 75% = 12GB of RAM utilized
Number of workloads × Average peak RAM utilization (GB) = Total peak RAM utilization (GB)
100 × 12GB = 1200GB of total RAM utilized

Accounting for growth:

Total peak RAM utilization (GB) x forecasted growth = Total RAM required

1200GB x 1.25 (25% growth) = 1500GB

> **Note:** The calculation does not include memory overhead requirements.

For this calculation, we assume the host has 256GB of RAM installed operating at 75% utilization.

RAM installed per host x Total host RAM utilization = Total RAM (MB) available.

256GB x 75% = 192GB

Total peak RAM utilization (GB) / Total RAM (GB) available = Number of hosts needed

1500GB / 192GB = 8 (rounded up)

Number of hosts needed + availability requirements (N+1) = 8 hosts will handle the compute workload.

Consolidating Processing Example Calculating the Consolidation from Three CPUs to Two CPUs[20]

This subsection provides a simple example of consolidating two servers into one. We need to calculate the CPU utilization and memory that is required when we move all applications and workloads onto a single server. From our baselining tasks, we learn that Server 1 and Server 2 have an average peak CPU utilization of 45% and 16%, respectively.

---

[20] Hertvik, Joe. Admin Alert: Making Educated Guesses on CPU Utilization. 9 January 2008. http://www.itjungle.com/fhg/fhg010908-story03.html

We need the formula in the following figure to help us predict the resultant CPU utilization for the single consolidated server.

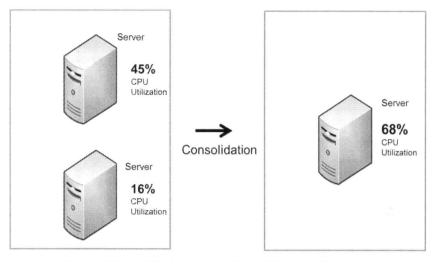

Note: 45% + 16% does *not* = Consolidated utilization!

Figure 39 Server Consolidation Processing Example

Calculations for Server Consolidation Processing Example

((CPU time / elapsed time) / number of processors) = average CPU utilization

CPU utilization = .45 (45 %)

Number of processors = 3

Elapsed time = 300 seconds

We need to solve for CPU time, which is an unknown value. Once I plug these numbers in, my equation now looks like this:

((CPU time / 300) / 3) = .45
CPU time / 300 = (.45 * 3)
CPU time = (.45 * 3) * 300
CPU time = 405

Once I know what the CPU time is for these particular values, my solved equation looks like this:

((405 / 300) / 2) = .68%

What this tells us is that the CPU peak utilization jumps to 68% percent if all the applications and workloads are on one consolidated server.

> **Note:** You do not get the correct answer if you just add CPU utilization values! (45% + 16% = 61%).

CPU Configuration and Design Considerations[21]

Remember, there is a difference between CPU usage in the physical and virtual world. Applications are scheduled by the OS in the physical world and mapped to specific CPUs. In the virtual world, each VM makes requests of virtual CPUs that are scheduled by the hypervisor virtualization software.

Also, with some virtualization solutions such as VMware, there is the concept of reserving resources from the host server for specific VMs. A reservation is a guarantee on the availability and use of either memory or CPU for a VM. For memory, it is a guarantee to access a certain amount of physical memory for the VM. However, if the VM is configured for 10GB of memory with a reservation of 5GB, the host server uses a swap file of 5GB (memory from the disk) if the host server is running low on memory. Accessing the disk for memory has a huge performance penalty.

For CPU reservations, there is a guarantee of CPU clock cycles. If a VM is not using its reserved CPU clock cycles, they are not wasted, because other VMs are allowed to use them. There is also the concept of "limits" for memory and clock cycles for VMs. Configuring memory and CPU limits can be dangerous. For example,

---

[21]David Davis & Alex Rosemblat. vCPU Sizing Considerations. July 2012. Web. http://www.vkernel.com/files/docs/white-papers/vcpu-sizing-considerations.pdf

if you set the memory limit lower than the configured memory for a VM, it causes swapping to the disk and performance suffers. For CPU clock cycle limits, you need to be careful since you could limit the performance of the VM if extra clock cycle capacity happens to be available.

Application Redesign

Some applications *cannot* operate in the cloud without some modifications, because cloud scalability is typically obtained by adding additional VMs *horizontally*. Because any new spun-up VMs cannot read the unshared local file system, horizontal scaling cannot be performed for legacy applications that have a habit of writing information and transaction states to their local file system during operation. This means these applications can only scale-up *vertically* by adding more CPUs, RAM, and IO. Vertical scaling can only go so far, but horizontal scaling can go on forever (well, that's an exaggeration, but it can go much further than vertical scaling). Scaling horizontally requires VMs to be identical, and each one must be capable of being terminated at any point.

The following figure illustrates the differences between vertical and horizontal scaling.

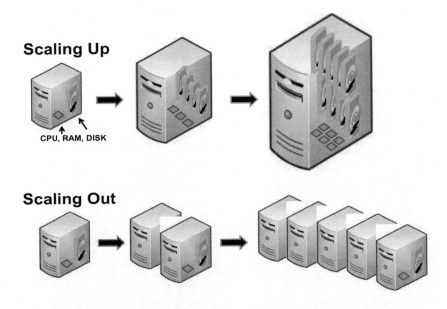

Figure 40 Scaling Up Vertically vs. Scaling Out Horizontally

Table 13 on the next page shows the limitations with legacy applications. During the design phase, applications with limitations need to be redesigned and coded before they can be migrated to the cloud. In addition to code changes, the application needs to be reconfigured to run in the new cloud environment. You need to identify any and all application configuration related files. If file paths or database login credentials have changed, then you need to update them in the application at the destination VM in the cloud.[22]

---

[22] Pooch. Application Migration Best Practices. 23 November 2013.
https://wsmintl.com/blog/application-migration-best-practices/

While the first concern is to ensure the problem applications are redesigned, coded, and configured, the next concern is to ensure they perform as expected. It is very important that the level of service and overall performance of the migrated applications are as good as or better than the original performance achieved outside the cloud. Failure to properly meet performance expectations could result in potential loss of business and higher costs, which negates any benefits of the cloud.

Table 13 Examples of Why Existing Applications Do Not Work in the Cloud

Network	
Migration Problem Area	**The Fix**
Applications using hard-coded IP addresses.	Use the host names and DNS to resolve the IPs (try not to use hard-coded IPs).
Original environment relying on specific holes to be open in firewall(s).	Ensure that the public cloud has firewall(s) configured to provide the necessary access.
Application requires very low latency across the network.	Design application VMs must be in close proximity to each other. Also ensure sufficient bandwidth and throughput are available on the public cloud.
	vSwitches do not enable a network monitoring tool to see internal paths for application performance monitoring.
Multiple network interfaces are not currently supported by some cloud vendors.	Import using a single virtual NIC, and use DHCP for address assignment. Add other interfaces manually after migration.

Network (Cont.)	
Migration Problem Area	**The Fix**
Domain Controllers (DCs) are typically set up with static IPs, which may be problematic to import to a cloud provider. Also, the nature of DC software and domain membership is such that trying to launch a Windows image with preinstalled and preconfigured Active Directory (AD) software is going to be problematic.	Install the DCs from scratch and join them to the original domain over a VPN. You must then replicate the AD databases and decommission the original DCs.
VM Compatibility	
Migration Problem Area	**The Fix**
VMware VM Disk (VMDK) files do not import into the public cloud.	You can only import VMDK files into some public clouds using their tools if the VMs were created through the OVF export process in VMware. You cannot easily export an instance from some cloud providers unless you previously imported it from another virtualization environment.
VMs created by a Physical-to-Virtual (P2V) migration sometimes do not work (a cloud provider like AWS may not officially support P2V migrations).	Rebuild servers directly in the cloud provider's environment.

Storage	
Migration Problem Area	**The Fix**
Application requires high Input/Output Operations per Second (IOPS)	Use the high-throughput IOPS design for IaaS in the public cloud. *Note:* AWS has the I2 series of compute environments (EC2) that provides fast SSD-backed instance storage optimized for very high IOPS.
Importing a VM with more than one disk is not supported by some cloud providers.	Use migration tools (Racemi, PlateSpin, etc.) to import the VM with only the boot volume, and import any additional disks later.
Very large storage devices (more than 1TB) are not directly supported by some cloud providers.	Emulate the disk storage using RAID 0, NAS. *Note:* Performance will be impacted by this workaround.
Solutions that utilize shared storage may be hard to forklift migrate since there are no direct equivalents in some cloud providers.	You can try creating a dedicated VMs as the iSCSI targets, or using AWS Storage Gateway[23]. *Note:* The performance may suffer because of the additional level of indirection for disk access.
Systems	
Migration Problem Area	**The Fix**
Application requires frequent and voluminous access to an on-premises database that cannot be migrated to the cloud.	Move the web front-end to the cloud only. Leave the application and database servers on-premise.
Applications run on legacy platforms that are not supported by cloud providers.	Do not move the application to the cloud.

---

[23] Forklifting to AWS: An Option for Migration to AWS. October 2014.
http://www.trinimbus.com/wp-content/uploads/2014/11/Forklifting-to-AWS-Whitepaper-October-2014.pdf

Data	
Migration Problem Area	**The Fix**
The application data store is not partitionable. Only one VM can process the information. (The data store partitions should be able to be replicated on other nodes to achieve redundancy.)	Modify the data store so it is partitionable. If the data grows in a linear fashion, it can be split into different chunks that can be serviced by different VMs.
If the application database uses a linked server concept to interact with another database, it cannot be moved to the Windows Azure SQL database.	Use the Windows Azure Virtual Network feature.[24]
Some third-party class library/frameworks are not supported by Azure.	The library needs to be modified or re-written.

Application and Operating System (OS) Software Licenses

If you do not use the software licenses provided by your CSP, you will probably have to move some or all of your existing licenses across to your provider. Carefully track your software licenses or you could end up paying twice for licenses.

Choosing a Contractor to Help Migrate to the Cloud

Migrating to the cloud requires full-time dedicated resources. No matter how you look at it, your IT team still needs to carry out the day-to-day tasks to run and support your IT systems. How will they find the time to plan and execute a migration to the cloud? The answer is, they won't. You will need to get extra help if you want to be successful. The resources can come from within your

---

[24] Mindtree White Paper. http://www.mindtree.com/sites/default/files/mindtree-whitepaper-migrating-an-existing-on-premise-application-to-windows-azure-cloud.pdf

organization or from outside consultants and contractors. You can choose the best option that makes sense for your organization.

If you choose help from the outside, then you need to do your due diligence to ensure you are getting experienced and proven contractors who actually know what they are doing. By now you may have noticed that many IT service companies have jumped on the cloud bandwagon and have suddenly become cloud experts overnight. Choosing a truly knowledgeable and experienced, cloud-managed services provider is not easy. What are some of the important criteria that a government agency should consider when choosing a contractor to migrate, operate, and support their applications in the cloud? The following provides a sample list of evaluation criteria.

1. **Experience:**
   - Have they solved real-world IT problems when migrating to the cloud?
   - What were some of the issues and how did they solve them?
   - What are the names of the organizations and companies that they have helped in the past?
   - Do they understand your mission/business and do they have the right mix of experience in the areas that are important to you?

2. **Standards and/or Community Development:**
   - Are they or have they ever been involved in defining cloud standards or contributing to cloud open-source communities?

3. **Interview:** I recommend performing a series of pointed interviews. Questions include:
   - Is their cloud migration methodology documented?
   - Do they have the business and technical savvy you are looking for?
   - Does their culture fit with your organization?

4. **Cost:**
   - Are their rates competitive?
   - Have you included their services cost in your ROI calculation?

5. **References:**
   - Contact the references that they provide.
   - Again, ask pointed questions.

   Remember, a consultant is only as good as his or her last job.

6. **Do they eat their own dog food?** This is one of the most important criteria that everyone forgets to ask. (This is a slang term referring to whether you do what you're prescribing to others. The real origin of the term is unknown. Some say it refers to the president of Kal Kan Pet Food, who was said to eat a can of his dog food at shareholders' meetings[25].) So, ask the question, "Do you operate your own company within the cloud?" (and I am not talking about simple websites). Here is a true story that illustrates this point:

   Years ago, I experienced an embarrassing moment when working as an engineer for an IT services company (name to remain anonymous). The company VP was in the final stages

---

[25] Harrison, Warren (May–June 2006). "From The Editor: Eating Your Own Dog Food". IEEE Software (IEEE) 23 (3): 5–7. doi:10.1109/MS.2006.72.

of convincing a government CIO that we were the best company that can deliver asset management and tracking of their IT assets.

He was almost done with the demo when the CIO pointed to a computer in the company's conference room and said "Is that your computer? The VP said yes. The CIO promptly stood up, picked up the keyboard, looked at the monitor, and computer and asked "Where are the barcodes? How do you track your own IT assets?" Ooops. Lesson learned. Again, don't forget to ask a services company if they "eat their own dog food."

Deploy Phase

Now that you have completed the first two "Discover" and "Design" phases of the migration methodology, you are ready to deploy your applications to the cloud. Before any applications are migrated, make sure you have a recent backup of all servers and databases. It also goes without saying that any application development activities should be suspended until the migration project is completed.

Remember that during the Design phase, the applications were sorted into groups based upon their complexity with respect to moving to the cloud. The applications were also redesigned if they had any limitations listed previously in Table 13.

To help fine-tune your migration steps and provide hands-on training to the migration and operations team, it is always good to first do a pilot using a simple application. You should gather feedback from end users and stakeholders so that improvements can be made before other applications are migrated to the cloud. A simple application like a website that doesn't have much connectivity or integration with other applications and databases is a good choice for moving to the cloud first.

Once the application migration processes have been proven, the more important and complex applications can be tackled. Throughout the Design phase, there should be a series of check point and review meetings. The design can be verified that the features and capabilities can be directly traceable to the RTM. After the pilot application has been migrated, tested, and operational, other groups of applications can be migrated and tested in a phased approach.

Plan and Schedule

A clear rollout plan must be developed that defines what is to be delivered and over what time period. The schedule should be tough, but achievable. Enterprise architecture programs can be easily delayed by politics and day-to-day firefighting, so the program manager needs to stay on his/her toes. One thing to remember, management is not patient. If no visible results are seen within 4–6 months, the program could be shut down.

Key Planning Tasks

1. Write a granular step-by-step script/checklist of what you need to do to for the migration.
2. Plan for database dumps and outages. Create a snapshot of your user data right before the applications and infrastructure are brought down for the migration.
3. Set the DNS TTL to less than 300 seconds to give you the chance to quickly roll forward and/or backwards if anything happens.
4. Assume almost everything will fail, and document backup plans and steps required to recover from any failures.

Types of Migration Deployments

The Forklift and Hybrid methods are the two main topics in this section that will be discussed for migrating to the cloud. Each type has its pros and cons, so choosing the right one depends upon your risk tolerance and factors specific to your environment.

Forklift Migration

A forklift migration deployment consists of moving major portions of the data center to the cloud all at once (hence, the term "forklift"). If you are moving into a private cloud data center, the actual servers can be physically "forklifted" and moved all at once. If the environment is virtualized, the VMs can be moved to an external hard drive and transported to the new cloud data center. Most of the time, however, a forklift migration entails moving just the applications. Application types that fit well with a forklift type move include self-contained web, low-small dependency, and tightly-coupled, multi-tier applications.

With a tightly-coupled application, only extremely low latency connectivity is required between the application tiers (web server, application server, and database server). The applications do not function properly if the tiers are separated over the internet or other Wide Area Network (WAN) that inject additional latency.

If you are lucky, moving the applications all at once may require no (or few) code changes. Moving the application typically involves reinstalling it from scratch in the cloud environment or importing/converting the existing VM into the new cloud environment. Other configurations such as setting up security groups, changing IP addresses, DNS, etc., need to be performed.

The first phase of the forklift move might not be able to take immediate advantage of specific cloud features such as elasticity, redundancy, load balancing, etc. These features can be added and configured later after testing has been completed.

Even before the second phase of the migration is performed, you are still shrinking the IT infrastructure footprint, which reduces costs over time. Like all migrations, you must have a written back-out strategy that can be used in the event things do not work properly during the move.

Hybrid Migration Strategy

Hybrid clouds are created by bridging a public/private cloud with your existing data center, which allows you to get the best of both worlds. A hybrid migration consists of taking parts of an application and moving them over time through a VPN connection to the cloud. The other parts of the application remain in place. The hybrid migration method provides a lower risk approach, since pieces of the application remain inside the existing network boundary preserving established connectivity and processing. It is also easier to revert back to the existing environment since you are moving applications in phases.

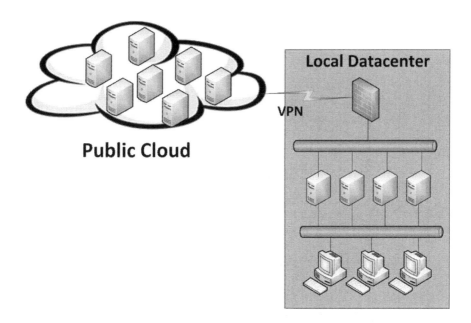

Figure 41 Hybrid Cloud Example

Although a hybrid approach allows you to stay within the same network boundary, components moved to the cloud will most likely be on a different network subnet. This means the VMs hosting the applications will need different IP addresses. In addition to IP address changes, you may need to code and test temporary software "wrappers" to allow the application components to communicate between your traditional data center and the cloud. A VPN connection must be established between the data center and the cloud, since it provides a secure "pipe" that isolates other traffic from interacting with your network traffic.

Some cloud providers allow VPN connections through the internet or via a direct connection into the cloud provider. The following table lists the cloud providers and associated carriers that provide direct connectivity to the cloud.

Table 14 Cloud Providers and Carriers Supported

Cloud Provider	Direct Connect Carriers
AWS	Equinix, IX Reach, Level 3, Tata Communications, Telx, Verizon, Zayo, etc.
Google Cloud	Equinix, IX Reach, Level 3, Tata Communications, Telx, Verizon, Zayo, etc.
Microsoft Azure	AT&T, Level 3, Verizon, British Telecom, SingTel, Orange, IIJ, Tata Communications, and Telstra.

Migration Tools

When moving an existing application to the cloud, you can either reinstall the application, OS, and associated software as a VM, or use software that performs what is called a P2V or Virtual-to-Virtual (V2V) conversion using software. Each method has its advantages and disadvantages. Most system administrators prefer to rebuild servers from scratch in the cloud when possible to prevent migration issues. Although this method tends to be more reliable, it is more labor intensive. A better method for large migrations is to use a P2V or V2V tool since it is faster and avoids human error.

The P2V Process

The P2V process consists of taking a physical system and converting it to a VM. This process includes creating one or more virtual hard disks. For the conversion process to work, the P2V process must replace the hardware device drivers so that they match the physical server hardware contained in the cloud.

> *Note:* The hardware change may require reactivating some of your software.

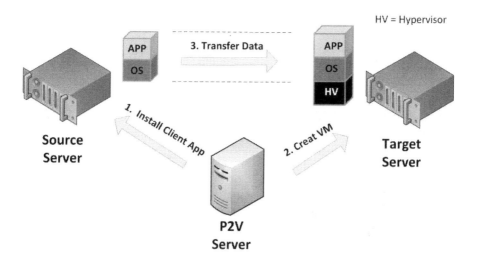

Figure 42 Illustration of P2V Process

VM Conversion Tools—VMware vCenter Converter

VMware offers both a free stand-alone version of its Converter product, and a version that is a plug-in to vCenter. VMware Converter can convert physical computers running 64-bit versions of Windows Server 2008, Windows Server 2003, and Linux (RHEL, SUSE, and Ubuntu). This tool also supports conversions from all VMware VMs, Microsoft Virtual PC, Microsoft Virtual Server 2005, and Microsoft Hyper-V VMs when imported as a physical source.

> *Note:* The VMware Converter only supports VMware VMs as a destination.

PlateSpin Migrate

PlateSpin Migrate is platform-agnostic, and can convert physical server systems to multiple virtualization formats (P2V). It can also convert between multiple virtualization formats (V2V) such as Hyper-V, VMware, and Citrix Xen, or it can go the other way and convert VMs to physical machines (V2P).

Unlike other converters such as VMware vCenter Converter, PlateSpin Migrate requires a multi-server installation. Although some people may consider the more complex, multi-server installation a disadvantage, once completed, it does not require agents to be installed on all of the source and target servers. PlateSpin uses Internet Information Services (IIS) and either a SQL Server or SQL Server Express database. The product is managed by the PlateSpin Migrate Client.

Conversion migrations can take a long time to complete, depending upon the network and storage system I/O speed. For example, for a localized conversion, a Windows system with a 250GB hard drive takes about 4 hours to convert over a 1Gbps Local Area Network (LAN). At the end of the process, the VM will boot up and the OS will automatically recognize the virtual device drivers. Conversions to remote cloud providers can be performed over WANs. Since WAN speeds are typically slower than 1Gbps, a conversion of 250GB or more will take more than 40 hours to move across a 100Mbps WAN to a cloud provider. Therefore, for large VMs, it is better to copy them locally to an external hard disk drive. The hard drive can then be shipped to the cloud provider who will transfer the VMs locally to the cloud.

Racemi

Racemi is a software tool/service that automatically migrates existing physical or virtual servers into the cloud or between cloud providers using software agents installed on the migrated host. This tool basically captures an "image" of the live physical server or VM that is planned to be migrated to the cloud, and automatically creates the target VM in the cloud environment. The images are encrypted using 256-bit SSL encryption for outbound HTTPS connections.

Microsoft Migration Tools

Microsoft has the Microsoft System Center VM Manager (VMM), App Controller, and Migration Accelerator software tools that facilitate migration to the cloud. VMM and App Controller work together and are used to move VMs from existing Hyper-V environments into Microsoft Azure. App Controller lets you manage the applications deployed on the VMs, and looks at the specifications of the existing VMs and recommends the minimum size to get the same or better performance in Azure.

After configuring the new VM in the Azure environment, you simply click the **Deploy** button and let it run. Depending on the size of the VM and the available bandwidth, it can take anywhere from minutes to several hours to copy the VMs into Azure. Once the process is complete, the VM automatically starts and is available for use.

Another Microsoft tool that automates cloud migration is Migration Accelerator. This tool is designed to migrate VMs away from a VMware virtualized data center or AWS cloud into Azure. Migration Accelerator has an automated discovery feature that helps identify VM workloads and proper migration scenarios.

Migration Accelerator requires the installation of a software agent on the target system. The agent is responsible for data synchronization and source image capture between the target system and Azure destination. In addition, a process server is installed and configured in the target environment, which establishes communications between the software agent and the destination VMs on Azure. The process server provides caching, queuing, compression, encryption, and network bandwidth management.

A third component of a configuration server is installed and configured on Azure to manage the communications between the target system and the Migration Accelerator portal. Lastly, a migration engine on the portal conducts the needed discovery and migration from the target host into the Azure VMs.

Testing

Once an application has been migrated to the cloud, assigned an IP address, the database(s) is restored, and the application is configured, it is time for functional testing. Connection to the VM can be performed the first time by using its IP address. To use the host name, you need to update the host name/IP address contained in the local hosts' file contained on your computer. (Updating the local hosts file is necessary since the DNS server has not been updated with the new host name/IP address.) Once connected, testing can be performed on the cloud application to confirm that the application is functioning properly.

Determine Phase

As discussed in the Deploy phase, the applications should be migrated in a phased approach with a small set of applications being turned up and tested at a time. After functional testing has been performed in the earlier phase, some measure of performance testing should be performed. The deployment team must "determine" if the application meets all SLAs, as well as customer performance expectations. Key performance metrics that were recorded during the baseline measurements in the Discovery phase should be compared to the performance exhibited in the cloud environment. Any major deviations (good or bad) in the cloud environment should be fully investigated.

Why is the Determine Phase important?

The goal is to have your IT infrastructure available 100% of the time. *Determining* the outcome of the cloud migration and ongoing operational performance is not a short-term project—it is a continuous improvement task. There are always some amount of errors or disruptions within the new cloud environment. Since IT services are used continuously, monitoring and support must be performed repeatedly.

ITIL V3 has a "7-Step Continual Service Improvement Process" that can be leveraged for the Determination phase of cloud computing environments.

The following figure illustrates the process flow:

Figure 43 ITIL V3's 7-Step Continual Service Improvement Process[26]

Step 1: What should be measured?

The first step in the process is identifying Key Performance Indicators (KPIs) such as availability, end-to-end response time, etc. KPIs are performance metrics that are linked to a strategic mission or business objective[27]. KPIs provide quick insight into trends and the current state of the cloud environment, which allows you to see how well it is doing and where it requires improvements. KPIs should be well defined and tightly linked to the agency or business' success or failure.

---

[26] ICCLAB. 11 July 2013. http://blog.zhaw.ch/icclab/how-to-apply-the-7-step-continual-service-improvement-process-in-a-cloud-computing-environment/
[27] Becher, Jonathan D. Mitigating Metrics Madness: How to Tell KPIs from Mere Metrics. http://www.cutter.com/content-and-analysis/journals-and-reports/cutter-it-journal/sample/itj0604c.html

All KPIs are metrics, but not all metrics are KPIs. An agency or business can have many metrics, but should only have a few KPIs. KPIs should be quantifiable and actionable. If you can measure it but can't change the outcome, then it is not a KPI. In general, KPIs are:

- Monitored frequently - Issues can be identified and corrected early.
- Outcome-oriented - Measured against a goal or best practice.
- Assigned to an owner.
- Target-based - Has a time-sensitive target value.
- Rated/graded – A measured metric can be compared to the target value.

The above criteria ensures that the focus stays on items that truly matter to the success of the agency or business.

Step 2: What can be measured?

Once you have a list of KPIs, you should consider how they are to be measured. For example, the end-to-end response time can be measured using software tools such as Riverbed, Wireshark, AppDynamics, and Compuware APM. Availability can be measured by periodically polling cloud resources. The polling can detect any outages and availability can be measured.

Step 3: Gather Data

Once the performance metrics have been defined, you should determine how and when to collect the data. You need to determine the following:

- Should the measurement be performed once per day, hour, or minute?

- Is the measurement frequency consistent, and is it taken during the same time frame?
- Should the data be collected by aggregating logs or by polling cloud resources?

Step 4: Process the Data

In this step, the data is aggregated and analyzed to create meaningful information. Depending upon the KPI, the data is averaged, summed, or tallied. Examples of how to gather and process data are shown in Chapter 4, "Baselining Performance."

Step 5: Analyze the Data

The processed data can be seen as a statistical sample with maximums/minimums, averages, standard deviations, etc. Analyze the data and see if it differs from the KPI values.

Step 6: Present and Use the Information

The data should be presented and interpretations extracted from the results. Are there underlying performance or security issues? If so, corrective actions need to be performed within the cloud environment. The underlying root cause of problems should be found (a root cause is a cause that once removed from the problem fault sequence, prevents the final undesirable event from recurring).

Step 7: Implement Corrective Action

The last step in the process is performing corrective actions. Since the Determine phase is essentially a continual improvement process, this final step completes the cycle loop and sets up the next cycle. Problems discovered during the continuous improvement process within the cloud environment should be corrected as soon as possible.

5. Conclusion

Congratulations, you are now properly equipped to migrate your IT enterprise to the cloud! This book discussed what cloud computing is, the details of how it works, and described a proven methodology (The 4 D's) of how to get there. The 4 D's (Discover, Design, Deploy, and Determine) migration methodology is explained in detail so that you can use it as your roadmap to migrate to the cloud. This book is one of the few books that actually dives deep into the theory and operation of cloud technology, and provides you with a full understanding of what the cloud is and how to leverage its benefits. Remember, you cannot manage something you do not understand.

In addition, I described some of the "gotcha's" and pitfalls in Table 13 that many people make when they try to migrate to the cloud. Now that you know these pitfalls and recommended remedies, you are sure not to repeat them during your cloud migration. I also discussed some of the software tools to help you discover what is really in your current IT enterprise environment and what performance metrics you are achieving. This discovery is important because a solid baseline helps you compare the performance and costs from the beginning to the end.

I explained how you can create a cost benefit analysis and a TCO analysis. I included standard templates for this analysis so that you can quickly lay out your calculations. These factors will facilitate your analysis and help justify your decision to migrate to the cloud.

So where do you go from here? What does the future hold for cloud computing? The title of this book is "From the Beginning to the End," so where is the end? If I look into my crystal ball, not only do I see a massive increase in adoption of cloud computing by federal/state agencies, DoD, and commercial companies, I see new technologies that will move us to the next level. These new technologies are a little foggy, but I believe new virtualization technologies such as containers, advancements in processing, storage, and security are on the horizon. Do not be left behind—it is time to be a successful leader and move to the cloud.

Made in the USA
Columbia, SC
20 November 2020